Praise for *Abiding in Amen*

Do you know how to pray? In *Abiding in Amen*, Wesley W. Ellis uses personal stories and his own struggles to remind us that prayer is not something to master or another thing to check off our to-do list, hoping that God is listening. Rather, prayer begins with God as we relinquish control, give up our desperate search for outcomes, and receive the gift of God coming to us. Prayer is a relationship with the Divine where we are called to wait, dwell, and allow the living God to act. Gleaning wisdom from Andrew Root, Harmut Rosa, and Richard Rohr, among others, Ellis uses the image of abiding to describe a relationship with God beyond our control as God comes to us. Abiding in "Amen" will require trust and even perhaps a paradigm shift, moving beyond prayer as a discipline to prayer as relationship. Ellis includes prayer practices at the end of each chapter, inviting individuals or groups to cultivate attentiveness to God. Ultimately, this is a book of hope and good news. A God who so loves the world indeed loves us too, and wants nothing more than to share the love of the living Christ with us.

—Marti Reed Hazelrigg, pastor of Oak Ridge Presbyterian Church, Oak Ridge, North Carolina

Wesley W. Ellis is one of the great young theologians working within the church and leading a congregation. In this book Ellis lives out this vocation on every page. This book is soaked with a mind and life that lead people into deep theological reflection by teaching them to pray. This is an exciting work.

—Andrew Root, professor and Carrie Olson Baalson Chair of Youth and Family Ministry, Luther Seminary, and author of the Ministry in a Secular Age series

How do we pray when belief itself feels fragile? In a world where certainty has crumbled and prayer often feels like an obsolete relic, *Abiding in Amen* offers a fresh vision of prayer—not as a means of control, but as an act of radical trust. Drawing on theology, philosophy, and lived experience, Wesley W. Ellis invites readers to rediscover prayer as abiding rather than striving, as resonance rather than performance. With deep pastoral sensitivity and intellectual rigor, this book speaks to those who wrestle with faith in an age of doubt, showing that true prayer is not about mastering techniques but about resting in the unshakable presence of God. This is a deep and encouraging book.

—John Swinton, FBA, FRSE, FISSR, RMN, RNMD, professor in practical theology and pastoral care,
The School of Divinity, History, Philosophy & Art History,
King's College, University of Aberdeen

ABIDING IN AMEN

ABIDING IN AMEN

Prayer in a Secular Age

WESLEY W. ELLIS

FORTRESS PRESS
MINNEAPOLIS

ABIDING IN AMEN
Prayer in a Secular Age

Copyright © 2025 Fortress Press. All rights reserved. Except for brief quotations in critical articles or reviews, no part of this book may be reproduced in any manner without prior written permission from the publisher. Email copyright@fortresspress.com or write to Permissions, Fortress Press, PO Box 1209, Minneapolis, MN 55440-1209.

30 29 28 27 26 25 1 2 3 4 5 6 7 8 9

Library of Congress Control Number: 2025003837 (print)

Cover image: Origami dove made of white paper on white plain background, from Pavel Abramov via iStock / Getty Images
Cover design: Ashley Muehlbauer

Print ISBN: 979-8-8898-3352-9
eBook ISBN: 979-8-8898-3353-6

To my church family

Contents

Acknowledgments

Before anything else, I must thank my incredible wife, Amanda. Her unwavering support, boundless love, and tireless care sustain me daily. She's the one who believes in me when I struggle to believe in myself, who holds our family together with grace and strength, and who loves Bonnie, Henry, and me with a depth at which I can only marvel. Amanda, this book is as much yours as it is mine—thank you for standing by me through the late nights, the long days, and the moments of doubt. You are my partner in every sense of the word, and I am endlessly grateful for you.

To Bonnie and Henry, my two little visionaries, thank you for teaching me how to see the world with fresh eyes. Your curiosity, unguarded joy, and tough questions continually reshape my understanding of what is true, good, and beautiful. You remind me to keep searching for wonder and hope. This book was written with you in mind because you help me remember that prayer is not about answers but about connection.

To my beloved church family at First Congregational Church of Ramona, this book is dedicated to you. You have nurtured me in more ways than I can count. Thank you for teaching me to pray. You have taught me to pray in the messy, ordinary moments of life, and it is in the context of your love and support that the ideas for this book took root and grew.

I owe a special debt of gratitude to Andrew Root, whose work has deeply influenced my own. The subtitle of this book—*Prayer in a Secular Age*—is a direct nod to his scholarship and ability to illuminate the complexities of faith in our time. He has inspired me to think deeply about the relationship among prayer, presence, and resonance.

I am grateful to those who graciously read early drafts of this book and offered invaluable feedback: Michael Paul Cartledge, Dolores Mortier, Jim and Linda Hogue, Alison VanBuskirk Philip, and Erin Raffety. Their thoughtful critiques and kind words helped shape this work into what it is now. All the faults of this book are my own, but I owe thanks to these folks for all its strengths.

A heartfelt thank-you is also extended to Laura Gifford, Chantelle Gibbs, and the brilliant team at Fortress Press. Their guidance, expertise, and patience were instrumental in bringing this book to life. Laura's careful attention to detail and ability to draw out the best in my writing made all the difference.

I am also indebted to the network of pastors in the Ramona community and the wider United Church of Christ. Mother Hannah Wilder, Kristie Grimaud, Larry Hand, Johnny Diaz, Holgie Choi, and Greg Davis have been incredible gifts through their friendship and collegiality. Without the support of my network, I am not sure I'd be in ministry at all, let alone writing books about it. This book could not have been written without the inspiration and encouragement found in shared ministry with these incredible ministers. I am also deeply indebted to Justin Forbes for his constant encouragement. In this regard, every good work of theology is a group effort, and I am profoundly thankful to be part of such a supportive community.

Finally, a word about why this book was written. As a pastor, I have encountered so many people for whom prayer has become a source of anxiety rather than joy. They feel they are doing it wrong, or that they are not praying enough, or that they do not know how to find the right words. Compassion for those struggles and the conviction that prayer should be a source of joy, not fear, are at the heart of this book. I believe that prayer is about abiding in the "amen"—dwelling in the resonance of God's love and presence—and I hope this book can help others rediscover the beauty and simplicity of that truth.

Introduction

Amen

I'd like to make something clear from the outset: This is not a book about how bad it is to be secular. And it is not a book preoccupied with the apparent decline of the church in America, in power or in size. Secularization, in this book, is not a malevolent force, at least not intrinsically. I think that a lot of good has come from secularization. Modernity and secularization have led to advancements in human rights, scientific and technological progress, medicine, increased individual freedom, and the separation of religious authority from state governance, promoting a more pluralistic and inclusive society. It has created a space for Christians to deconstruct some of their inherited and embedded theologies, and it has even created the opportunity for the church to become humble, like Jesus, and divorce itself from the will to power and the allure of Christendom. I am not concerned here about people taking prayer out of schools, or posting the Ten Commandments in a public library, or waving an American flag too close to the pulpit.

Of course, conversations about these things may very well be important, especially considering the dramatic shifts that have taken place in America since at least 2016, particularly the shift toward Christian nationalism that has taken place in American Evangelicalism. I have a vested interest, in fact, because the tradition that seems to be anxious about these things is a tradition that has had a profound effect on my own spiritual formation (even though I would now comfortably consider myself a Mainliner as a minister in the United Church of Christ with a background working in Lutheran, Presbyterian, and United Methodist settings). There is certainly a well-documented anxiety in American Evangelicalism over the church's apparent loss of relevance and the specter of secularization swallowing up Christian faith altogether.[1]

But I am in no battle over the culture here, and I don't wish to express any interest in the church's status in society or its furtherance of Christian values in the ethical arena. Rather, my concern about secularization is theological. I don't suspect that we can or should necessarily desire to cease to be secular, and I certainly don't want to go back to some bygone era when people were still looking for demons around every corner and blaming mental illness on their parents' unrepented sin. What I am concerned about is not escaping secularization but exploring how we can remain faithful (and specifically Christian) *within* a secular age. We are all secular now. That is my contention. I do not wish to change this. Even still, I do believe it is possible to be faithful Christians. As James K. A. Smith has put it, "We don't believe instead of doubting; we believe *while* doubting. We're all Thomas now."[2]

But to remain faithful, I believe we need to think about which specific challenges we are facing, which epistemic challenges and cultural obstacles we are up against every time we turn to God in prayer. By *epistemic challenges*, I mean the basic challenges we face regarding knowledge and what counts as knowledge. The term *epistemic* comes from the Greek word *epistēmē*, meaning *knowledge* or *understanding*. In philosophy, epistemology is the branch that explores questions like: What is knowledge? How do we know what we know? What distinguishes justified belief from subjective opinion? An epistemic claim, for example, deals with the basis or justification for believing something to be true. The term *cultural obstacles* here refers to barriers that arise from differences in cultural values, beliefs, practices, or social norms that have emerged in late modernity and can prevent mutual understanding, acceptance, cooperation, or a shared narrative among people.

Make no mistake, we do live in a modern society. We face real epistemic challenges and cultural obstacles. Postmodernity's contributions to the epistemic landscape of modernity notwithstanding, we remain modern. And modernity is marked not merely by secularization as a subtraction of God from society but more profoundly by the introduction of the drive for controllability as the core value of all our social arrangements and the centrality of human agency in the quest to make the world attainable and useful. Human beings are seen, by modernity, as the masters of their fate, as the primary (if not sole) agents in history, and our relation to the world is one of being and becoming masters, more and more—to possess and control the world.

Hartmut Rosa, the German philosopher and sociologist, describes the project of modernity as one of making the world controllable. In his book *The Uncontrollability of the World*, he grasps for the correct term to describe this. Because he's thinking in German and trying to work his thinking into the English language, he laments the difficulty of translation. The German term *verfügbar*, which gets translated as *controllability*, has a variety of meanings in English. It can be understood as the conglomeration of the meanings of "engineerable, predictable, available, accessible, disposable in all aspects."[3] At a recent lecture at Princeton Theological Seminary in New Jersey, Rosa expressed his preference for the term *disposable* and suggested that maybe he should have "gone that way" in his book.[4] When we make the world controllable, it becomes "at our disposal," and we make it disposable. It can be used and even, eventually, thrown out. It's only an instrument, a thing. This, of course, has had very real consequences in history. Modernity has produced the disposability of things like fossil fuels and rainforests, such that we have created an ecological crisis to the point that we—the agents of history and the masters of fate—have potentially already doomed our world to oblivion. But as serious as those concerns absolutely are, my concern here is about what modernity, through secularization, has done to our understanding and relationship to prayer. Has Yahweh—the God of Israel, the God we Christians confess to be the one revealed in the crucified Jesus—become an idol? Has our drive for control and instrumentalism made God into a "thing," a commodity, and thus something at our disposal? Have we made God disposable?

Rosa's concept of *verfügbar* is central to his understanding of what plagues modern society and contributes to what Charles Taylor calls the "malaise of modernity"—the sense of disorientation and dissatisfaction many people experience in modern Western societies.[5] Taylor talks about how the radical individualization, the instrumental reason, and the loss of meaningful political engagement in modernity have created a sense of angst and even despair. From Rosa, we can infer that the main culprit behind this malaise is what he calls *social acceleration*.[6] He argues that as society accelerates—through faster communication, accumulation, technology, and the rationale of progress—there's an increasing desire to control and manage every aspect of life. However, Rosa suggests that despite these efforts, many aspects of life remain fundamentally uncontrollable, hence the malaise. This uncontrollability leads to a sense of alienation as people struggle to keep up with acceleration, feeling overwhelmed by unpredictability and the demand to achieve growth and progress.[7] Paradoxically, while social acceleration promises more control, it actually exacerbates experiences of uncertainty and lack of mastery, leaving people feeling disconnected from the world.

The need for acceleration has caused a frenetic compulsion to expediency, to make everything useful. This leads to the eventual objectification of reality. Rosa writes, "A fully engineerable world eventually would be a 'dead world.'"[8] Was Nietzsche right to say that "God is dead"?[9] Have we so commodified, instrumentalized, and objectified God that God comes to us now as a dead thing, an instrument of our own agency? According to Andrew Root, "Faith that has become certain is no longer (by definition) faith; it has become idolatry, where we no longer seek out a living personal God but make this God into a frozen idol."[10] In my experience as a pastor, in praying and discussing prayer with so many people, I believe this is how it feels to many who pray. They wonder why prayer isn't "working" for them. They struggle because one cannot have a relationship with an idea, and we've made God into an idea. They wonder why they don't feel they've "mastered" the "discipline" of prayer. So these questions about secularization are not posed to a secular *them*, outside of Christianity, but to the faithful (myself included) who pray—perhaps even regularly—but are often confronted with the feeling of a dead, frozen object instead of a living God.

I fear that in this secular age, prayer itself has become disposable. Under the force of modernity, even the most spiritual people are at risk of making prayer into a means to an end, a technology to be engineered and optimized for (if we're really spiritual) the growth of our faith or (if we're so persuaded) the acquisition of the things we ask for in our prayers—"God, please help me get a job or find a really good parking spot!" It's not so much that we *don't* pray, that prayer has been disposed *of*, that worries me; it's the very notion that prayer may be at our *disposal*. Prayer, co-opted by the optimism of modernity, has become one more thing for us to control. It is this disposability of prayer, and the disposability of God, that brings me to these pages.

The opposite of *verfügbar*, in German, is *unverfügbarkeit*. *Uncontrollability*, like *controllability*, is not the only word we could use to describe the "problem" that modernity is apparently trying to solve. The uncontrollability of the world, though a bane to the modern endeavor, is at the heart of prayer. We cannot control God. Prayer belongs not in the category of engineering but of relationship. Have you ever tried to engineer a relationship? You can't engineer a relationship without eventually engineering it to death. Eventually the manipulation is revealed, and the relationship becomes toxic. The good news is that whatever it is that we have engineered to death, it is not actually God. The "dead thing" is a false idol. The God of Israel, revealed in the crucified Jesus, is yet alive and therefore is not an object but a person. And, thankfully, this relationship, the love God has for us, is not dependent on our reciprocation. It is a relationship built on freedom and grace.

I AND THOU—HAVING AND BEING

To find some corrective for this modern push for controllability, it will help look at two important Jewish thinkers: Martin Buber and Erich Fromm. Both scholars offer insights that push against the objectification of relationships, inviting us to reclaim a sense of the personal and the sacred. Buber's concept of the "I-Thou" relationship challenges us to see God not as a distant idea or an object of knowledge but as a living, dynamic presence. Fromm, with his emphasis on love and the necessity of meaningful human connection, echoes this by implicitly suggesting that encountering God can be as intimate and transformative as truly loving another person. Together, their ideas encourage us to move beyond a detached, intellectualized faith and open ourselves to experiencing God as a person.

Martin Buber (1878–1965) was born in Vienna and raised by his grandparents after his parents separated when he was a child. His grandfather, a scholar of Jewish literature, greatly influenced his intellectual development and love for Jewish tradition. Buber became a philosopher and storyteller whose work centered on the power of genuine human connection. His most famous book, *I and Thou*, explores how deep, authentic relationships can transform us when we encounter others—even God—with openness and presence. Buber believed that life's most meaningful moments happen when we move beyond surface interactions and truly engage with one another, seeing the other as a "Thou" rather than an "It."

Martin Buber's concept of I and Thou contrasts two ways of relating to the world and others.[11] In the I-It relationship, we treat people and objects as things to be used, categorized, or understood from a distance. It's an impersonal, functional way of relating. In a word, it is instrumentalization. In the I-Thou relationship, however, we encounter others as unique, whole beings, engaging with them in a mutual, genuine, and present relationship. This interaction is sacred and transformative, where the other is not an object but a partner in dialogue. Buber emphasizes that true meaning and connection—what we may, with Rosa, call *resonance*—come through these I-Thou moments.

Erich Fromm (1900–1980) was born in Frankfurt, Germany, into an Orthodox Jewish family, which influenced his early intellectual and spiritual development. He pursued studies in sociology and psychoanalysis, eventually becoming a prominent social psychologist, humanistic philosopher, and psychoanalyst. Fromm's work combined Freudian psychoanalysis with Marxist social theory, and he explored the ways that society shapes human behavior, particularly in his famous books *Escape from Freedom* and *The Art of Loving*. He believed that modern society often leads people to feel disconnected and alienated, and he championed love, creativity, and freedom as essential to overcoming these struggles. After fleeing Nazi Germany, Fromm settled in the United States, where he continued to write and teach, leaving a legacy of ideas that emphasize the importance of human connection, self-awareness, and social responsibility.

Fromm's understanding of *being* and *having* parallels Martin Buber's concepts of I-Thou and I-It. For Fromm, the *having* mode is focused on possession, control, and the use of objects or people for one's own benefit, much like Buber's I-It relationship. It is a way of interacting that is materialistic and detached, where people and things are treated as commodities. In contrast, the *being* mode emphasizes authentic existence, creativity, and genuine connection, similar to Buber's I-Thou relationship. Here, individuals engage deeply with others and the world, experiencing life fully and authentically, valuing presence and mutuality over ownership or control.[12] Both thinkers highlight the transformative power of authentic relationships over utilitarian interactions.

If our quest for control has commodified prayer and our relation to God in such a way that God has become an *it* and not a *Thou*, if we are so in the *having* mode of action and existence, then we need somehow to find our way, through the labyrinth of epistemic challenges, to an I and Thou relationship of being. We need to move from the instrumental to the relational.[13] I suggest that the reason prayer has become a source of frustration and shame, rather than a source of joy and resonance, is that we have turned it into an instrument rather than a relationship. As Richard Rohr puts it, prayer has become a "technique for getting things, a pious exercise that somehow makes God happy, or a requirement for entry into heaven."[14] For Rohr, prayer is "more like practicing heaven now."[15] In his groundbreaking work *Resonance,* Rosa puts his thesis quite succinctly: "If acceleration is the problem, then resonance may well be the solution."[16] To all these issues of the deadening of reality through objectification and instrumentalization, and the apparent malaise that comes with them, Rosa offers a one-word solution, which he spends another 150,000 words to unpack. But what is resonance?

In Rosa's context, *resonance* refers to a deep, meaningful connection or interaction between individuals and the world. It involves a responsive and fulfilling relationship where people feel truly engaged and attuned to their surroundings rather than experiencing a sense of alienation or detachment. This concept emphasizes the quality of personal and social relationships and their impact on one's sense of fulfillment and well-being.

"THE DUDE ABIDES"

On a typical sunny morning in Ramona, I sat down at a local café for breakfast with a friend of mine, Jim, one of the members of my church. Jim is well-read, theologically motivated, and thoughtful. So he makes for a good dialogue partner. Every pastor needs a Jim.

As we sipped our coffee and nibbled on pancakes, we discussed Andrew Root and Blair Bertrand's book, *When Church Stops Working.*[17] We were trying to understand together what they meant by the term *resonance,* which they got from Rosa. More accurately, since Root and Bertrand do have good definitions in their book, we were trying to think of easy and more theological ways of explaining it to the folks in church whom we knew would struggle with the term's somewhat abstract nature. We delved into how resonance involves experiencing meaningful and fulfilling connections with others and the world. We searched for helpful illustrations. We talked about empathy, and both agreed that resonance seems to capture something essential about our spiritual and social lives, but we struggled to pin down a precise theological definition.

As we brainstormed, Jim's face suddenly lit up with a spark of inspiration. With a grin, he exclaimed, "The Dude abides!"—a nod to one of my all-time favorite movies, *The Big Lebowski*.[18] Jim's excitement was infectious as he connected the idea of *abide* from the Gospel of John to our discussion. In the film, *abide* represents an open and accepting approach to life, and Jim suggested this could parallel a theology of resonance.

The Dude, played by Jeff Bridges, is a laid-back slacker who lives a simple life in Los Angeles. Known for his casual demeanor and love of bowling, the Dude embodies a philosophy of nonchalance. His life takes an unexpected turn when he is ironically (and comically) mistaken for a wealthy namesake, essentially his opposite, who prides himself on his ability to pull himself up with his own work—by his bootstraps, if you will. Consequently, the Dude becomes entangled in a bizarre kidnapping plot involving a rug that "really tied the room together," some white Russians, green toenail polish, nihilists, and a sack of dirty undies.[19] Throughout the film, the Dude remains remarkably unfazed by the chaos around him, offering a comedic contrast to the more frantic characters (including his namesake) and highlighting themes of fate, identity, and the randomness, unpredictability, and uncontrollability (i.e., *unverfügbarkeit*) of life. Rather than trying to control the world, the Dude just lets life come to him.

It's important to note that the analogy shouldn't be taken too far. The Dude doesn't exemplify all of what we'd look for in Christian virtue. In fact, he's a very flawed character. But nevertheless, the Dude abides. He does not force anything. He doesn't approach life as a "point of aggression."[20] He doesn't "take control"; he just "lets things happen."[21] He doesn't put stock in his own agency. The Dude doesn't really seem to care much about agency at all. The stark difference between the Dude and the kind of abiding we need in Christian discipleship is that our abiding has a definite object (or subject) in whom "we live and move and have our being" (Acts 17:28 NRSVUE). And, unlike the Dude, Christians do anticipate bearing fruit.

MENO

In the Gospel of John, chapter 15, Jesus said to his disciples, "Abide in me as I abide in you. Just as the branch cannot bear fruit by itself unless it abides in the vine, neither can you unless you abide in me. I am the vine; you are the branches. Those who abide in me and I in them bear much fruit, because apart from me you can do nothing" (John 15:4–5 NRSVUE).

Jesus emphasizes the importance of remaining connected to him, using the term *abide* (Greek: *meno*) to describe this essential relationship. The key message of John 15 is that just as branches must stay connected to the vine to bear fruit, so must people remain in Jesus to live a spiritually "fruitful" life. Jesus insists that apart from him, individuals can do nothing, reinforcing the idea that true life comes from a continuous, abiding relationship with God and *not* from the constant exertion of energy and the effort to take control of the world. Life comes from God and not from human agency. Perhaps this is what Jesus truly meant when he told Nicodemus that he had to be "born again" (John 3:3 NIV).[22] One does not generate one's own birth by exercising one's own agency. Birth is something that *happens to* you. You cannot control it: "The wind blows wherever it pleases. You hear its sound, but you cannot tell where it comes from or where it is going. So it is with everyone born of the Spirit" (John 3:8 NIV). We cannot control God, and prayer is not a tool we wield. We have to let things happen; we have to abide in God. Prayer is not about getting God to work for us; prayer is resonance.

In exploring the concept of *abide* as used in John 15, it becomes clear that abiding in God is about resonance. It signifies a deep, authentic relationship with God rather than using God merely as a means to an end. The term *abide* suggests a persistent, intimate union with Jesus, marked by trust, commitment, and empathy. It is an I-Thou relationship, built on being and not on having. It is not about leveraging God for personal gain or achieving specific outcomes but cultivating a genuine, ongoing connection with God. This relationship is rooted in God's love and faithfulness, not our ability or inability.

It is a relationship of grace that can only be received, not compelled. Abiding also denotes a mutual indwelling, an empathy, where Jesus lives within his disciples, and they live in Jesus, *in Christ*. This mutual presence suggests a relationship that is both nurturing and empowering, ensuring that disciples are consistently guided and sustained by Jesus's teachings and presence. Prayer, then, is not a means to an end; it is being present and genuinely connected with the divine.

Abiding in Christ, letting Christ's work happen through and to us, and allowing space for God's agency, *not our own*, to determine our existence may give way to a *being-in-the-world* instead of the constant acceleration of control and the malaise that accompanies it. Abiding then provides the theological vocabulary for the concepts of the being mode (Fromm), the I-Thou relationship (Buber), and resonance (Rosa). In our secular age and in the midst of the malaise of modernity, the Dude abides, and so must we.

AMEN

As I mentioned above, however, I think there is an important difference between the way in which the Dude abides and the way that Christians are called to abide. The Dude seems to simply *abide*, but in what is he abiding? He doesn't really seem to abide *in* anything. We could stretch, perhaps, and say Bridges's character is abiding in the present moment, to which there may indeed be some deep spiritual significance.[23] But the point I want to make here is that disciples of Jesus do, however, abide *in* something (actually, someone).

Have you ever paused to reflect on that word we say just about every time we say a prayer? No, I'm not talking about *Lord*, or *God*, or *please*. And no, I'm not talking about *gimme*! I am talking about the word we say at the end—*amen*. What is that? Why do we say *amen*, other than for the obvious reason that if we didn't, nobody would know we were done praying?

The word *amen* originates from the Hebrew word *'āmēn*, which means *truly*, *certainly*, or *so be it*. In the Bible, it is often used to affirm something as true, to express agreement, or to seal a prayer with a declaration of trust in God. When we say *amen*, we are not merely closing a prayer; we are making a profound statement about God's authority and our relationship to it.

In Scripture, Jesus frequently uses *amen* (often translated as *verily* or *truly*) before key statements, such as in the Gospels when He says, "Amen, I say to you" (e.g., Matt 5:18; John 3:3). This usage reinforces the reliability and truth of Jesus's words, pointing to God's ultimate truthfulness and sovereignty. For us, saying *amen* goes beyond agreement. It signifies a surrender to God's will and an affirmation of the primacy of God's action, God's agency, in the very act of prayer. In prayer, *amen* is a way of relinquishing control and entrusting the outcomes to God. Indeed, in a way, it disregards outcome as the purpose of prayer. In saying *amen*, we are allowing outcomes to be secondary to the deeper relationship that is being experienced and acknowledged in prayer. *Amen* becomes a moment of abiding in God, relinquishing the need for control and declaring, "I trust you." Jesus said, "Come to me . . . and I will give you rest" (Matt 11:28–30). In prayer, in abiding in *amen*, we rest in Christ and look to God's action, not our own, as the determining and motivating element of prayer itself.

Thus, *amen* becomes an act of faith, a reminder that in every prayer and in every moment of life, God is the one in control (if control even continues to be a helpful category), and we are invited to abide in that trust. When we say *amen*, we are saying, "I trust you."

Therefore, by saying *amen*, we are confessing a desire to live into a reality that cannot be brought about through human agency, an end that cannot be reached through human means, a life that cannot be controlled or engineered and is therefore alive. We are abiding in the one who is and will be "all in all." God is not a means to an end. Our end is not reached *teleologically* but *eschatologically*—achieved not by human effort but through God's ultimate action. Prayer is an act, not of our becoming but of God's coming to us. Abiding in amen discloses resonance with God and with the world that God loves (see John 3:16). The following pages will explore and clarify this claim.

PRAYER AS ABIDING IN AMEN

Rosa writes, "If acceleration is the problem, then resonance may well be the solution."[24] My thesis here, though unpacked much less thoroughly and comprehensively than Rosa's, is similar: If instrumentalization is the problem, then abiding in amen may well be the solution. Of course, that's far too easy to say; clear definitions are required, and there are certainly problems with such a crude problem-to-solution thesis, but that is at least one way of saying what I am trying to propose here. I think Rosa, Root, Rohr, and others can help us understand how the malaise of modernity has made prayer exceptionally difficult for us, and I believe that by abiding not in our own understanding or agency but in amen, relinquishing control to and finding resonance with God, we can find hope and life and a God who lives. Thus, throughout this book, I will use the term *abide* to describe what I think John 15 is getting at: the overlap of what Rosa calls *resonance*, what Root calls *encounter* (in his early writing) or *waiting*, what Rohr calls *presence* or *union*[25]—all of which center on relationship as an end in itself, paradoxically soaked in hopeful anticipation, as God comes to us as we are with proleptic promise and *perichoretic* passion.[26]

I pray that this book will be a gift to all its readers, and especially to my church family at First Congregational Church of Ramona, the people who taught me to pray. I pray that this book will, if nothing else, take off some of the pressure and help people realize that they are not alone in their doubts, their struggles, or their crises of faith. And I pray that somehow, in the pages of this book, someone may find resonance and abiding in God. Amen.

A WORD ABOUT THE COVER

Before I conclude this introduction, I want to risk the unconventional and make a comment about the cover art for this book. As you may know, the extent to which an author of a book has any say on what goes on its cover is dependent on the publisher. I am grateful to Laura Gifford and her team at Fortress Press because they did consult me on my preferences for the cover of this book. I am no artist or art critic, however, so I was happy to provide just a little insight and then let the artists do their thing. Well, I am pleased to say that both aesthetically and conceptually, the artists at Fortress Press did not disappoint, but the commendation of the art itself is not the cause for my brief commentary here. Rather, I want to reflect on the symbolism of the paper dove because I believe it helpfully encapsulates the fragility of spirituality and the risk of the instrumentalization of prayer in a secular age, which represent my main concerns in writing this book.

The image of the dove is a powerful symbol of spirituality and transcendence due to its long-standing associations with peace, purity, and divine presence across various religious traditions. In Christianity, the dove represents the Holy Spirit, as seen during Jesus's baptism when the Spirit descended like a dove, signifying God's coming to the world into which Jesus has been sent. It symbolizes divine approval and connection with God. Its gentle, peaceful nature also embodies spiritual ideals of love, hope, and renewal, making the dove an all but universal symbol of transcendence and spiritual grace. In the Old Testament, the dove first appears in the story of Noah's Ark (Gen 8:8–12). After the flood, Noah sends out a dove to find dry land. When it returns with an olive branch, it symbolizes peace, hope, and the end of the invasion of watery chaos, marking a new beginning for humanity. It would be wrong to miss the connection between the deluge of the Noah story in Genesis 8 and the watery chaos of Genesis 1:2. In Genesis 1, the Spirit of God is depicted as "hovering" or "fluttering," like a dove, over the waters of chaos, anticipating the creation act of bringing harmony to the chaos through God's Word. In Genesis 1:6–8, God separated the waters from the waters as one of the first acts of creation. In Genesis 8, when the water from above meets again with the water from below, it symbolizes more than mere destruction; it symbolizes the undoing of the work of creation, threatening an end to the harmony. When Noah sends a dove out to find dry land, the dove signals the anticipation of the new creation and the hope for harmony that hovers again over watery chaos. This imagery of the dove carrying a sign of peace enforces the hope that even in the midst of the malaise of modernity, new creation is coming through God's action in prayer.

In the New Testament, as mentioned, the dove symbolizes the Holy Spirit, particularly during Jesus's baptism (Matt 3:16), where it signifies the presence of God's Spirit descending on Jesus. This trajectory is important. It is not Jesus clambering up to God; it is God's coming to Jesus, which, as we will discover in the following pages, is the proper trajectory of prayer. Together, these biblical stories weave the dove into a rich tapestry of spiritual themes, including peace, renewal, divine blessing, and the presence of God's Spirit, making it a deeply resonant symbol of spirituality even in a secular age.

Paper is the stuff of productivity and capitalism. On it, we print our money; we write schemes for investment plans and policy procedures. You may be reading this book on paper as a means to understand theological concepts and master a theological discipline. You may use paper to record your budget or write your grocery list. Paper is nothing if not *useful*. However, turning it into art or folding it into a dove undermines its typical utility. Hopefully, this book will undermine whatever utility modernity might have in store for prayer.

Finally, paper is fragile. One can easily crumple or tear a paper dove. In a secular age, prayer and the very notion of transcendence are fragile, not just conceptually because of their contested status in epistemology, but they also *feel* fragile.[27] In conversation after conversation, I have discovered the fragility of prayer in people's lives, the tenuousness of at least the rationale for faith, and the haunting of doubt that so many people in the world are feeling today.

To me, the image of the paper dove captures so many of the themes I hope to investigate in the following pages. I want to find in prayer the hope of the coming of God into our fragile and frantic worlds. I want to undermine the usefulness of prayer and elevate prayer as a work of resonance, a work that belongs primarily to God and only secondarily to us.

CHAPTER ONE

I Don't Know How to Pray

God wants to come down to us, God wants to come to us and we do not need to clamber up to [God], [God] wants to be with us to the end of the world.

—Martin Luther

JOHN AND REVEREND SARAH

John was a devout member of a small Presbyterian church in Virginia. Known by his friends as having a strong faith in God, he was a member of the Christian Education Committee at the church as well as a staunch proponent of the church's outreach in the community. He volunteered every month in the church's food distribution program and regularly helped with weekly worship gatherings by reading Scripture, leading prayers, and sometimes even preaching the sermon. John was also on the Hospitality Committee and was one of the first faces you'd see if you attended the church. He was one of those guys who just exuded faithfulness, and people saw him as a spiritual leader in the church.

Lately, however, John had been experiencing doubts and frustrations, especially concerning his prayer life. He felt he wasn't praying enough, and even when he did pray, he doubted whether his prayers were truly making a difference. "Is this even working?" he wondered.

"Is anybody listening? What am I doing wrong?" John noticed that every time he stopped to pray, he felt like he needed to begin by apologizing to God for not praying enough. The irony that he was praying even as he was apologizing for not praying wasn't lost on him, but nevertheless, he was struggling.

One day, as the sun dipped below the horizon, casting a warm, golden glow on the church's beautiful brown steeple and stained-glass windows, John decided to seek guidance from his pastor, Reverend Sarah. Sarah was just wrapping up her day, putting the finishing touches on her sermon and getting ready to go take her kids to the park with her husband for some family time. Sarah's office door was connected to the administrator's office and was open, as usual. After saying a quick hello to Bridget, the administrator, John walked straight over to Sarah's office and knocked on the door frame to let her know he was there.

"Hey, John! How are you doing today?"

Without answering, he walked into Sarah's cozy study, nervously fidgeting with his hands. "Can I close the door?" he asked.

Sensing that their conversation was about to be a sensitive one, Sarah said, "Of course" and reached to close it herself.

John found comfort in the familiar surroundings of the church office. He'd known more than one pastor who'd occupied the space over the years, and he knew it as a safe place to bring questions and receive guidance. But his doubts weighed heavily on his heart. As he began to share his concerns, his voice trembled. He was surprised at how nervous he felt. He was about to make a confession that felt somehow silly but also quite serious to him.

"Reverend Sarah," he began, "I feel like I'm failing. I am trying really hard to pray 'unceasingly,' like the apostle Paul tells us to, but I am really struggling to pray even once a day. I want to connect with God more deeply, but I always feel distracted and doubt whether my prayers are even being heard. I tried using an app to help me remember to pray, but I can't help but feel guilty. I don't know what to do. I know God is there—I think—but I just don't think my prayers are working. Am I doing something wrong? What can I do?"

Reverend Sarah listened intently, her face displaying genuine empathy. She knew the burden of doubt all too well, though she had kept most of her own struggles hidden from her congregation. After all, if people knew that she barely believed in prayer herself half the time, how could she expect them to trust her in leading them in prayer? She figured doubt was probably something she should keep between her and her therapist, at least for the most part. But seeing John's vulnerability, she felt it was time to open up.

"John," she said, her voice gentle, "I understand your feelings. Prayer is a profound and personal journey, and it's normal to encounter doubts along the way. Even as a pastor, I face my own struggles with prayer at times."

Surprised by her honesty, John looked up, meeting her eyes with a mix of relief and curiosity. "Really?" he asked, feeling a little less alone in his struggle.

Reverend Sarah nodded. "Yes, really," she replied with a smile. "It's human to question and doubt, but remember that faith isn't about having all the answers. It's about embracing the mystery and continuing to seek a deeper connection with God. Really, though, sometimes it seems that ministry gets in the way of prayer."

As she spoke, she started to feel a familiar sense of anxiety. Worried that she was about to say too much, she tried to make it positive and muster a sense of resolution. After all, John had come to her for help, not for her own venting.

"Through it all, I find solace in leaning on faith, depending on God's grace, and remembering that I'm not alone. We all have our struggles with prayer. You're not alone, John. You see," Sarah continued, speaking to herself as much as to him, "prayer isn't just about saying the 'right' words or spending a specific amount of time. And it's not about getting results. It's about a relationship. It's about opening our hearts and minds to God, even amid uncertainty. It's okay to express your frustrations and doubts in prayer too; God listens to our hearts. Just look at Psalms. If you want to cry out, 'Why have you forsaken me?' you're actually in pretty good company!"

Even as she said this, she doubted herself a little but knew it was true. She knew her prayers weren't futile. At least, she tried to know it.

As John absorbed her words, a sense of comfort enveloped him. He realized that he wasn't alone in his struggle and that even his pastor faced similar challenges.

* * *

I've had the privilege of serving in a variety of churches. Since my college years, I have served in an Evangelical church, Presbyterian churches, a couple of United Methodist churches, and a United Church of Christ congregation. I've also spoken at conferences and taught courses for seminarians and church leaders from across the Protestant theological and denominational spectrum. As a teacher, pastor, and youth worker in those various settings, I have had many conversations like the one Reverend Sarah had with John. Full disclosure: While that is formally a fictional story, it's based on true events. I know the feelings of doubt that even pastors and church leaders carry with them. I've heard testimony of the struggle that so many people have with prayer. Too often, those struggles are suppressed and hidden. Too often, they go unnamed.

I wish I could say that every conversation about prayer ends with even the minimal kind of resolution that John and Sarah found. Actually, it's up to you to decide if you think they found their resolution after all. Who knows how John may have felt just minutes after leaving Reverend Sarah's office? Who knows if his anxieties were really relieved? I have had countless conversations with people about their prayer life. In fact, in the days while thinking about writing this book, I made a habit of asking people—even people who had come to me for very different reasons—how their prayer life was going. I suspect that many people have left my office after those conversations feeling just as anxious and guilty as they did when they entered.

EVERYTHING FEELS OFF

I remember a conversation I had with a woman named Robin. One Sunday morning after church, as I was shaking hands with people as they exited the sanctuary, Robin pulled me aside and asked if she could come talk to me later that week. She wasn't comfortable telling me why right there, but I could tell it was important to her, so we made an appointment. When she came to my office a couple days later, she sat down in her chair and seemed to sink into it. The weight she was carrying on her shoulders was almost visible. In the incalculable moments between *hello* and *how are you?*, I scrolled through the possibilities of what she was there to talk about. Was she going to confess that she had done something terrible? Was she struggling with alcoholism? Had she been diagnosed with cancer? Was her husband cheating on her? Was she watching too much Fox News? It had to be something serious.

After pausing and releasing a breath, Robin confessed, "I don't know how to pray."

This was not what I was expecting. In fact, in the moment, it struck me as a fairly superficial problem, especially after all the buildup. After all, if you're this concerned about something, shouldn't it be a little more concrete than prayer? I mean, prayer is great and all, but it's not like food and water. We can survive without it, right? Why was Robin so upset by this?

This is part of the problem, isn't it? I mean, if I—a pastor and theologian—could think of prayer as superficial, then it's no wonder people struggle with it! We're pulled in two directions: by our undeniable thirst for a connection with God and equally by our suspicion that all this spirituality stuff is far too subjective to be taken too seriously. We're paradoxically cross-pressured by the importance and yet the apparent absurdity of the notion of prayer.

Catching myself in the irony of my own thinking, I asked Robin to tell me more.

"I want to feel connected to God," she said, "but when I stop to pray, everything feels off. I keep bouncing back and forth between wondering if anyone's listening at all, feeling like I must be doing something wrong, and getting distracted by other thoughts. I feel guilty because I am trying, but I know I am not praying often enough. And I feel insecure . . . like, I am a Christian and believe in Jesus, but I don't know why I feel like I am talking to the wall when I pray. Can you help me, Pastor?"

YOU'RE NOT THE ONLY ONE

Robin's story is representative of countless conversations I've had with young people, parents, church leaders, fellow pastors, and even church matriarchs (you know, the people in the church who have just always been there and seem to have unwavering faith). The most common feelings that people convey to me are feelings of guilt, insecurity, shame, and frustration. Surprisingly few people report that they are satisfied with their prayer life. If you think prayer is hard, you're not alone. If you feel guilty because you can't seem to master the most basic Christian practice, it's not just you.

I believe the difficulty of prayer has far less to do with your own effort, the depth or maturity of your spirituality, or the amount of work you put into it than you might think. You've got more than your own limits working against you. In fact, you have a tidal wave of social, epistemological, theological, and hermeneutical conditions that all make prayer a source of guilt and shame when it should be a source of peace and life.

There are so many books on prayer. Many of them are very good. I hesitate to suggest we need another one. But far too often, in most of the books we have on the subject, the challenges of prayer that we are facing today are left unaddressed or in the background. The greater influences of secularization that are conditioning our experience are mostly ignored. So the guilt and shame are implicitly preserved, suppressed, and perhaps even subtly stigmatized. Even when reading some of the best thinkers on prayer, we find it far too easy to infer that we really just need to try harder. If we can just devote more time to prayer—if we can just exert a little more effort—then we'll be real "prayer warriors." In many of the beautiful theologies of prayer that have been offered to us through various mystical perspectives, monastic traditions, and pastoral and practical theologies of the church, few have diagnosed the issues we're currently facing in our secular neoliberal society, so many seem to be treating the wrong symptoms.

PARADIGM SHIFT

I think we need a paradigm shift. Now, I don't take that phrase *paradigm shift* lightly. It does get tossed around a lot, doesn't it? A paradigm shift is a profound and fundamental change in the way people perceive, think of, or approach a particular practice, concept, theory, or field of knowledge. It involves a shift from one established way of thinking, understanding, or doing things to an entirely new framework or perspective. When we say *paradigm shift*, we often really just mean an addition—adding a new thought onto an established thought. But a paradigm shift isn't like addition; it's not even like multiplication. It's more like realizing we've been doing math when we should have been doing poetry.

When we think of prayer, we tend to think of something that people do. It's a "discipline" that mature Christians must "master," right? Well, I think that's wrong. We need to think about prayer from an entirely different position. As Karl Barth puts it, "Prayer is a grace, an offer of God. . . . We are in the position of persons who can only receive."[1] Prayer is not something *we* do, at least not primarily. Prayer is, first and foremost, something God does. It is "the freedom of the Word and of the Spirit."[2] Prayer is a practice in the register of grace, not effort. Therefore, we can't expect to address our prayer struggles with more effort or better programs or more expedient church administration or the expenditure of more energy. The problem is *not* that there is "not enough," so the solution is *not* "more." The problem, as I will attempt to show, is one of what Hartmut Rosa calls "resonance" and what Scripture has called "abiding" (*yâshab* in the Hebrew Scriptures and *menō* in the New Testament)—waiting for, dwelling with, and finding our being in God rather than in our own understanding and achievement. What's required is a reversal in the trajectory of prayer, from God to us instead of from us to God. Prayer does not come from us; it comes *to* us.

This has not always been grasped by our pastors, denominational leaders, theologians, or even many of our mystics. For example, Stanley Grenz, one of the great Baptist theologians of his generation, rightly pointed out that prayer tends to play second fiddle to other church concerns such as pastoral counsel, church administration, youth and music ministries, Christian education (this concern being significantly marked by the fact that the traditional Wednesday prayer meeting has been replaced in many churches by a Wednesday night Bible study), and, of course, the budget: "When was the last time that prayer was given top priority at any denominational sponsored meeting or in any denominational promotion? Denominational programs readily target a variety of urgent tasks. Alas, prayer is rarely among them."[3] Grenz was right back in 1988 when he penned these words, and I think they're pretty spot on right now too. Grenz diagnosed the problem quite well and says it better than I could: "When it comes to prayer, denominations and churches are simply reflecting what is true of individual Christians. For many believers, prayer is a lost art. Many do not know how to pray and do not pray. For many of us, prayer is a source of guilt. The mere mention of the word results in an immediate recognition of our personal failure to pray as we should. Rather than being the source of feelings of joy and victory that it is intended to be, for most of us prayer triggers a sense of guilt and defeat!"[4]

Grenz got this right. But then he moved on to do some math when he should have done some poetry. After offering this excellent diagnosis, he jumped right into talking about that Wednesday night prayer meeting—wouldn't it be great to get that back?—and "small groups." He saw the problem of prayer, but his first thought was about human action and, ironically, better church programs. He remained in the from-us-to-God paradigm. But this is not a problem that can be solved simply by bearing down and praying harder or giving people more and better opportunities to pray. It's not a problem we can solve with more or better church programs or by "motivating the people of God to pray," as Grenz saw it.[5] In fact, I believe our struggle with prayer is one that can be solved not by doing more of anything but by letting things happen to us. It will require our getting out of the way, waiting, and allowing the living God to act.

Prayer comes from God, not from human beings. Thus, the paradigm shift I think we need—especially in light of the tidal wave of secularization that's already broken over us—is to allow the first thought of prayer to be God's action. Of course, secularization not only necessitates this shift, as I hope to show, but also makes it more difficult. How can we look first to God's action when the notion of the existence of God has become a contested thought? But precisely because human action has replaced divine action in the epistemic landscape of American Christianity, prayer has become a source of exhaustion and frustration. Our only way out, as it turns out, is to wait on the very God we've come to doubt. God must get us out of this.

This is not merely an abstract concept. The paradigm shift should not only be in the ether of dogmatic speculation. It cannot merely be a thought experiment. This change in our theology must meet the ground of our actual experience and emerge from it. It must be a practical theology—one that insists on the theological reality of all human experience. It must emerge from the way we engage and experience prayer and, more to the point, our intimacy with God. This is why we must begin from the ground of our experience, to investigate our experience so that we can name the mystery of our lived encounter with God. This is why it's so important that we begin with confession.

PRAYERS OF CONFESSION

As with most mainline churches in America, in our worship gatherings with my little United Church of Christ congregation in Ramona, we almost always share in a prayer of confession.[6] And it's usually pretty early, if not right at the beginning of the worship liturgy. It goes something like this: "Most merciful God, we confess that we have sinned against you in thought, word, and deed, by what we have done, and by what we have left undone. We have not loved you with our whole heart; we have not loved our neighbors as ourselves. We are truly sorry and we humbly repent. For the sake of your Son Jesus Christ, have mercy on us and forgive us; that we may delight in your will, and walk in your ways, to the glory of your Name. Amen."[7]

Or it could sound more like this: "We do not presume to come to this your table, merciful Lord, trusting in our own goodness, but in your unfailing mercies. We are not worthy that you should receive us, but give your word and we shall be healed, through Jesus Christ our Lord. Amen."[8]

The confession, thankfully, is followed up by an assurance of pardon, read or said by whoever is leading the liturgy. In my experience, if the prayer is appropriately introduced and prayed in earnest, the assurance comes as a breath of fresh air or a deep exhale: "We can rest assured in this: Our God—the God revealed in Jesus Christ—is a God of mercy and love, who greets our confession not with condemnation, but with grace and forgiveness. Praise God! In Jesus's name, we are forgiven!"[9]

Even after years of following this pattern, sometimes I still get goosebumps as we say the prayer and as we anticipate the assurance of pardon. It's a collective experience. God is forgiving the sins of the world, not just my own individual sins (though those too). It is the confession of God justifying, by grace alone, the whole human family and all creation. As I sometimes remind our congregation, confession is not something we do because God may punish us if we don't. Confession is not a mechanism for the compulsion of guilt. It's about God healing relationships that have been broken. It's about God restoring us from the brokenness caused by others. It's about God accepting us as we are. Perhaps most importantly, confession is about removing whatever masks we may be wearing to hide our truest selves.

For me, it's one of the most meaningful elements of the worship liturgy, but I realize that not everybody is a fan. For some people, the idea of confession conjures up the feeling of compulsory guilt. Perhaps they are recovering from religious trauma, from theological traditions that emphasize the threat of eternal damnation or purport an image of an angry God—possibly rooted in a flat-footed "sinners in the hands of an angry God" theology. For them, confession may be a source of restriction and pain. Or maybe they are victims of the sins of others, bearing the trauma of abuse or discrimination, and the confession of *their* sin, in light of the sins they've suffered, seems hardly a healthy thing to do in a worship gathering; perhaps it's even traumatic. If confession were only about the admission of guilt and the securing of a pardon, then one might conclude that confession may be more harmful than helpful. But that's not all confession is about.

Recently, I was commuting home late at night. I had been out with a couple of friends at a San Diego Padres baseball game. I had dropped off my friends at their cars and was by myself for the last twenty-five minutes of my forty-five-minute commute. I was feeling uneasy with myself. Do you ever feel that? Just sort of *off*? It may have been because the Padres had just lost in heartbreaking fashion, but it probably had more to do with a combination of other things.

Earlier that day, I had announced a new ministry initiative to the council at my church. I was excited to share about the endeavor. Our church had been chosen to take part in a new collaborative ministry project aimed at ministering with young adults, a demographic that my church (as with the church at large in America) is hemorrhaging. This would be an opportunity for us to explore what God is doing in the lives of the young adults of our community, and with the support of other churches, this surely would be a catalyst for our church. The announcement was received with some brief excitement, but the expediency questions immediately started getting asked: "How are we paying for this?" "How is this going to grow our church?" "Why are we spending money so haphazardly?" "This wasn't in the budget!"

I had adequate answers for all the questions, I think, but was still troubled by my own insecurities: Don't they trust that this is worth the cost? Don't they see that this is why we have money in the first place? Don't they trust my judgment as their pastor? Do they think I'm just throwing money around? Are they second-guessing my leadership? Do they see me as irresponsible?

Of course, this is my own baggage, not really that of the church. The questions were actually warranted (even if they could have waited for a different forum, maybe after we had the chance to celebrate what God was doing in our church). Even still, all day, even during the baseball game, I was distracted, fighting off my feelings of insecurity. Not only that, but I had just dropped off my friends and realized that I had been dominating the conversation while we were driving. I do that too much. I get excited and just talk way too much, and right after the conversation, I feel bad about it. It happens all the time, unfortunately. My friends keep coming back, so it must not be as big a deal to them, but to me it feels icky.

So, left with my own thoughts, driving up the hill to Ramona, I was feeling uneasy. I was feeling a little ashamed of my social inadequacies and insecure about my leadership and the trust of my congregation. In summary, I was just down on myself. But it occurred to me that I should take some time to pray. At that moment, the confession I needed was not one of guilt. The real problem was not my "fault"; it was my shame. I think a confession of my inadequacies as a leader would have been redundant. I didn't need forgiveness per se. I needed acceptance. I needed reassurance. So my prayer of confession that night was simply this: "God, I just need to hear that I'm okay right now."

Sometimes that's the best we've got. Sometimes the confession we need is to simply be honest with ourselves about our needs. To sit in our need and wait for God to meet it—for God to come and meet our guilt with forgiveness, our brokenness with healing, and our shame with acceptance.

Confession, then, is not only God forgiving us for our sins, the sins of which we ourselves are guilty as individuals. It's also about

God accepting us when we're struggling to accept ourselves. In the car that night, I needed to be reminded that I was okay, that I was not a bad pastor or a bad friend. So I confessed my need to God. I would have loved for someone to speak a word of assurance to me (and that's why I am so grateful for the assurance of pardon in the liturgy). That night, the quiet of my car and the music of Derek Webb coming from the stereo would have to suffice. And while I didn't see a vision of the Spirit descending like a dove or hear a loud voice saying, "With you I am well pleased" or anything like that, my confession gave me the space to wait for God, and I began to feel a little better.

As it should be in our worship liturgies, confession is about *honesty* with self, with others, and with God. As such, confession is a wellspring of freedom and joy. We are free to fully be ourselves, with the volume up, free from all the expectations that burden our souls. And we find joy in the revelation of God's delight in us just as we are. Confession invites us to loosen our grip on the world and admit that we don't have everything under control. In our confession—just as the father of the so-called prodigal son ran to greet his youngest with a ring, a robe, and a party (Luke 15:20–24)—God greets us, whether we are perpetrators or victims, with gentleness and humility (Matt 11:28–30). This is why our worship liturgy includes and often begins with confession. When we have embraced the vulnerability and joy of confession, we can embrace the gospel itself, the good news that all are loved and welcome in Christ's commonwealth.

The starting point of this book is the confession that prayer has become more difficult for us, in our secular age, because its meaning has become distorted for us. Indeed, our very understanding of the God to whom we pray has become distorted for us. It's not merely that secularization has made it more difficult to believe in the existence of God. It is because secularization and the underlying epistemic and philosophical positions it has birthed (or perhaps from which it has been birthed, depending on how you look at it)—neoliberalism, capitalism, instrumental rationality, burnout, and developmentalism—have shifted the ground on which we stand and contorted the vantage point from which we pray, skewing our understanding of the very purpose, trajectory, and *telos* of prayer. There are ways we have contributed to that change (maybe we should just name it as *sin*), and there are ways we have been made its victims. But as perpetrators, victims, or mere observers, let us confess. Let us be honest with God and with ourselves that we need prayer that meets our uncertainties and heals, rather than exacerbates, our felt inadequacies and failures. We need prayer that meets us in our being and not our becoming, that finds us as we are and not merely as we *should* be. We need prayer that anticipates God's coming to us and not our clambering up to God. We need. That is where this all begins.

Abiding in Confession

Confession is not about perfect words or polished prayers; it is about simple honesty before God. Sometimes the very act of wanting to pray is itself the prayer. Confession, at its heart, is the admission of our need—our need for God, our need for grace, our need to surrender what is broken inside us, even when we can't name what that is. There are times when we simply don't have the words, when the weight of life feels too heavy, or when the chaos inside us leaves us speechless before God. This, too, is prayer.

In moments like these, the "Spirit intercedes with groanings too deep for words" (Rom 8:26). Confession becomes a space for silence, for stillness, for simply being present. It is a sacred act of acknowledging our limitations, admitting that we are at a loss for words, but still desiring to come before God. And in that desire, we confess something deeper: that prayer does not depend on our ability to articulate or understand. Prayer is about our dependence on God's action, God's presence, and God's grace, which work even when we cannot.

Here's how you might enter a prayer of confession, even when words escape you:

1. *Sit in Silence*
   Begin by finding a quiet space. Breathe deeply and let yourself settle. There is no rush, no need to force words. Just be still in the presence of God, acknowledging that you are here, and so is God.
2. *Acknowledge Your Wordlessness*
   Offer up your wordless desire to pray. You might say something like, "God, I don't know how to pray right now, but I want to. I don't have the words, but I know you hear my heart." Or it could be something like my prayer in the car after the Padres game: "God, I just need to hear that I'm okay right now." Let your lack of eloquence be your confession, trusting that God is already at work, even in your inability to speak.

3. *Surrender Your Feelings*
   If there is any heaviness, confusion, or longing within you, release it to God. You don't have to explain it or understand it; just let it be what it is, trusting that God understands what you cannot express. Trust that God's grace reaches into places you cannot name, bringing healing and hope where only silence lives.
4. *Listen for God*
   After sitting in the silence of your confession, take a moment to listen. You may not hear words but listen for the peace that comes from knowing that God is with you, even in your silence. Listen for the gentle reminder that God's action, not yours, is what holds you.
5. *Rest in Grace and Say "Amen"*
   Finally, rest. Confession is not only about what we offer to God but also about receiving God's grace in return. Trust that your inability to speak does not hinder God's love for you. Let the grace of God hold you, even when words fail.

When you say "amen," know that you are surrendering—abiding in God and acknowledging that the outcome is in God's hands, not yours. Amen is a way of letting go, of entrusting yourself to God's ongoing work in you, beyond what you can say or do. It is a declaration that God is the one who finishes what we cannot, and that is enough.

Amen.

CHAPTER TWO

Prayer Is Not a Matter of Fact

In my experience as a pastor, people are sometimes surprised to discover that my own spiritual journey is fraught with doubt and uncertainty. I sometimes feel the need to apologize for it because I think it can be unsettling for people to learn that their pastor—the one who is supposed to be the *most* spiritual and lead them in their own devotion to God—has not figured it out. But as unsettling as it may or may not be, in my experience, it has been fruitful for me to be honest with my church family. Confessing my own doubt has opened space for the people I serve to be honest with themselves and to realize that doubt does not need to be an emergency. In fact, doubt may be an important element, if not a central element, in the journey of faith and discipleship. Allowing this space has enabled them to trust that even when they're not certain anyone is listening when they pray, it'll be okay, and perhaps they'll feel God's presence next time. My hope is that they can discover, as I have, that we lean not on our own understanding but on the grace of God (see Prov 3:5–6). In our prayer of confession the Sunday prior to this writing, our confession went like this:

> God of everlasting kindness. We confess today that we have struggled to be faithful to you. Indeed, many of us find it difficult to even believe that you exist. We wonder if anyone hears us when we pray. But God, in

our doubt, grant us assurance of your love. Heal our unbelief. Embrace us where certainty has failed us. Grant us a fresh faith so that we can rest in your presence. Grant us hope, even where there seems to be no hope. Fill us with your Spirit and be our strength in weakness. Let us find freedom in your forgiveness and grace.

This prayer was followed by this assurance of pardon: "We can rest assured in this: Our God is loving and merciful. We stand not on the strength of our own belief or on the certitude of our understanding but on the fullness of God's grace that surpasses understanding. In Christ we are welcome, and we are accepted just as we are." It's important for us to confess that doubt is the atmosphere around us. Doubt is uniquely pervasive in our world, in part because we've bought into ways of knowing that aspire to certainty. Prayer eludes certainty.

DOES PRAYER EXIST?

One key reason that prayer is difficult for us is that we can't know it, at least not from any objective vantage point. More precisely, prayer is difficult because it does not fit into our modern categories of knowledge. Not only are we unable to acquire any certainty of its effectiveness, but we also don't even know if prayer exists. That may seem like a silly claim. Objectively speaking, there is a thing that people do that they are content to call *prayer*. They bow their heads, fold their hands, or something like that, and they think, say, or read words that are directed to a deity or deities of some kind, the existence of whom/which, however, is unverifiable and hotly contested in our society (not to mention in our own minds). There are countless books that have argued, some more persuasively than others, the nonexistence of God. From Bertrand Russell's *Why I Am Not a Christian* to Richard Dawkins's *The God Delusion*,[1] it is no longer unheard of to argue against God's existence. In fact, it seems that the burden of proof, as it were, has been placed squarely in the court of the theist and not the atheist. But people still pray. Sometimes they do it in a worship gathering, sometimes in private. As a human activity, we know prayer is a thing.

It seems to me that most books about prayer are primarily interested in the human activity, the thing that people do, the thing we can observe. But prayer, theologically understood, is not merely a human activity. If it is prayer, it means that God is active (and in order for God to be active, God sorta has to exist). As Andrew Prevot has put it, "God is not merely the addressee of prayer but its primary agent."[2] So the question persists: Does prayer exist?

What we cannot know, from the vantage point of scientific evaluation or objective certitude, is if anything is actually happening outside the immanent categories of biology, psychology, or physiology during those times when people do that thing we call *prayer*. Nor can we prove that God is coming to us with the grace of prayer. That is, we cannot objectively observe the more pressing and urgent definition of prayer: a relational encounter, a resonance, between human beings and the divine. In a biblical theology of prayer, we must assert that prayer involves not only human beings and their action but also God and God's action. For prayer to be prayer, it requires God to act in some way—to listen, speak, be attentive. In fact, in a biblical understanding of prayer, that divine action is and must always be *primary*. "Strictly speaking," Sarah Coakley writes, "it is not I who autonomously prays, but God (the Holy Spirit) who prays in me."[3] So while "prayer" is a thing, of course, on the human side of the equation, the question is still open: Does prayer happen when people pray? Does prayer exist? In order to affirm that prayer exists, you have to operate outside our typical categories of knowledge and embrace the transcendent. You must look to a larger horizon than in objective knowledge and natural laws. Prayer cannot be grasped. Prayer grasps us.

THE PROBLEM OF KNOWLEDGE

From a theological perspective, we have an epistemology problem—a problem with what we regard as knowable and what we consider to be an adequate account of reality. There is something problematic about what we think it means to "know" something. I mentioned that the existence of God is hotly contested in our society. This is true, but it hasn't always been so. In his 2007 tome *A Secular Age*, Canadian philosopher Charles Taylor took on the ambitious task of explaining how we moved "from a society in which it was virtually impossible not to believe in God, to one in which faith, even for the staunchest believer, is one human possibility among others."[4] In only 851 pages, Taylor gives a compelling explanation, if not just a little suspicious in its tidiness. There are many contours of this process of secularization that Taylor gives himself room to explore, one of the most important being a sense of the self in a secular age.

Following the early development of the dualism of the interior self and the exterior world, which Taylor charts in his other important book *Sources of the Self*, the meaning of the exterior world gradually shifted more and more in the direction of what we now call *objectivity*.[5] We became observers, ascribing meaning to things from a detached and shielded position. In other words, we created a boundary between ourselves—our understanding of the self—and everything else, moving the meaning of things exclusively to the location of the mind. Taylor calls this modern development the "buffered" or "bounded" self, a contrast to the premodern conception he calls the "porous" self, which "straddles" the boundary between self and the exterior world.[6] "As a bounded self," Taylor explains, "I can see the boundary as a buffer, such that the things beyond don't need to 'get to me,' to use the contemporary expression . . . This self can see itself as invulnerable, a master of the meanings of things for it."[7]

The default position, then, becomes one wherein we understand ourselves as able to step away from things and observe them for understanding: "The buffered self is essentially the self which is aware of the possibility of disengagement."[8] We are not the subject of things; rather, things are objects for our use, dissection, measurement, examination, and (eventually, we hope) certainty. If we come across something we do not understand, we can roll up our sleeves, put on our lab coats, and get to work on it. What we do not know is merely what we do not *yet* know. Reality is ever before us, a puzzle to be solved, without reference to interventions from supernatural forces (even if we believe that God, in some way, created the puzzle): "The immanent order can thus slough off the transcendent."[9]

According to Taylor, "Instrumental rationality is a key value" in this *new* understanding of the self.[10] The external world is a world of resources. These resources are objects to be used, mined, burned up, spent for the benefit of the buffered self. "Modern thinking," writes Jürgen Moltmann, "has developed by way of an objectifying, analytical, particularizing, and reductionistic approach. The aim is to reduce an object or fact to its smallest possible, no-longer-divisible components, and from that point reconstruct it."[11] Moltmann goes on to explain, "The concern and methods of this kind of thinking are directed towards domination of objects and facts."[12] We solve the puzzle, we master the discipline, we possess the knowledge, we dominate nature. Everything becomes an instrument of our own self-actualizing achievement, identity construction, and teleological development.[13]

As Andrew Root has pointed out, the concept of the self in modernity ("modernity's man") represents an "upward conflation" of reality with human rationality. Root writes, "it conflates human instrumental rationality with reality so fully that it sends human consciousness to the top as ruler of reality and, as I would add, falling into the primal sin of upwardly conflating the creature as the creator."[14] We see this played out in Manifest Destiny, the ecological crisis, and developmental psychology. We see it in the industrial exploitation of the earth and in five-step plans for achieving spiritual maturity. Thomas Merton wrote, "There are some men for whom a tree has no reality until they think of cutting it down."[15] Everything exists so we can use it. This is the water we swim in, and even the water exists so that we can swim in it!

In a secular age, though transcendence is not evacuated or replaced, its promises are substituted by those of the industrial society and its vision of the future. For Moltmann, this is existential and points to a larger problem concerning our relationship to time. In other words, this represents an eschatological problem. To protect ourselves from the essential "unsayability" of the future—its uncontrollability, mystery, and imperfection—we, as Richard Rohr puts it, "attempt to build for ourselves many protections . . . we search for predictability, explanation, and order to give ourselves some sense of peace and control."[16] The concept of "future" has been made to mean the same thing as "goal" so that "present" (as well as the things that occupy the present) is reduced to "means."[17] Time, and our understanding of the future, suffers the same fate as transcendence itself. It is no longer determined by the coming of God or the will of a deity; instead, it is the instrument of progress and the process of maturation. According to Moltmann, "Today the understanding of 'future' suffers the same fate [as transcendence]. On the one hand, 'future' in industrial society was identified with the progress and development of the present status quo. 'Future' was objectified in the growth-rate of social products and the acceleration of the objective potencies of a man [*sic*]. As long as the industrial system found itself in the process of construction, its objective progress exuded the fascinating spell of transcendence."[18]

Thus, whether you consider industrial society the cause or the effect of secularization, it has tried to substitute transcendence with efficiency and mystery with objectivity. This substitution has certainly had some effects worth celebrating (I like running water and depression medication as much as the next guy), but its effects on our ability to be present in the moment and our relationship with nature have been regrettable, to say the least.

Moltmann, among others, has pointed out the damning effect this instrumental rationality has had on ecology. Indeed, the priority of industrial efficiency is a root cause of the ecological crisis in which we now find ourselves. According to Moltmann, in our secular society, "we know something to the extent in which we can dominate it. We understand something if we can 'grasp' it."[19] We have condemned our natural world to death for the sake of capital gain. We condemned creation because we sought to use it rather than know it. And now, in our alienation from our Mother Earth, we face the existential threat of her uninhabitability. In Moltmann's words, "Knowledge, as the Hebrew word tells us, is an act of love, not an act of domination."[20]

This buffered self, with its instrumental objective rationality, ultimately forms what Taylor goes on to refer to as "the immanent frame," or "closed world structures." It is a frame of knowing and an account of what knowledge is that both "encloses" the immanent and "boxes out" the transcendent.[21] The frame of reference is the buffered self, protected in its natural interiority, holding within it the meaning that had once been perceived to exist external to the self. Thus, the world and things are understood as instruments of the self, valued according to their usefulness to the self and its actualization.[22] The immanent frame is indifferent to things that lie outside of the sphere of usefulness and productivity, especially things that constitute true mysteries that cannot be solved but only experienced. While the buffered self represents an "upward conflation" of reality with objective and instrumental reason, the immanent frame also (perhaps paradoxically) represents a downward conflation of all reality with immanence. In a sense, the modern perspective is agnostic about even the existence of reality outside of what we can use. Ours are "the only minds in the cosmos,"[23] and our minds are the "master of the meanings of things."[24]

THE WORLD IS SECULAR, AND SO ARE YOU!

Others have done the difficult and important work of unpacking Taylor's explanation of the buffered self, notably James K. A. Smith in his much more accessible (and much shorter) book *How (Not) to Be Secular* and Andrew Root in his "Ministry in a Secular Age" series. I refer you to their important work for a fuller understanding of Charles Taylor's philosophy. And, of course, you can go read Taylor for yourself. But for our purposes, we should understand that the immanent frame is our cultural and intellectual milieu inside and outside the church. It is the framework in modernity where people understand and experience life primarily within a self-sufficient, natural order without reference to God or the transcendent. It describes a context in which meaning, purpose, and moral values are explained and pursued without recourse to the divine, emphasizing human flourishing within the limits of the material world. While it doesn't necessarily exclude belief in God, it shifts the focus to human-centered, secular explanations, making belief one option among many.

Borne in the immanent frame is an aversion to, or at least a suspicion of, what John Swinton and Harriet Mowat have called "ideographic" forms of knowledge, which focus on the particular and emphasize detailed, in-depth understanding of unique events, individuals, or contexts. The immanent frame's emphasis on a self-sufficient, natural order favors knowledge that can be quantified and generalized, often leading to a preference for nomothetic forms of knowledge. Nomothetic knowledge, which seeks universal laws and prioritizes objective, broad patterns, aligns with the secular, human-centered focus of the immanent frame, as seen in the natural sciences or large-scale social studies.[25] We will tolerate subjective experience as anecdotal, but we prefer hard data and "useful" information: "So-called 'soft' forms of knowledge such as spirituality may have their place, but they are only allowed to eat at the table after the hard sciences have finished their meal."[26] Subjectivity is interesting, perhaps, but objectivity and fact rule the day. Elsewhere, I have referred to this preference for hard science as the "empiricist regime" in epistemology.[27]

We must understand that the empirical appetite for objectivity and empiricism is not limited to the spaces outside of religion or the church. Indeed, by this understanding, the world is secular—and so are you! There is a temptation to set up a dualism of church and "the world," as though the church existed outside of the world that God so loved (John 3:16). This temptation has its genesis in some of the language of Scripture. The apostle Paul, for example, does set up precisely such a dualism in some of his letters for strategic purposes. In Romans 12, he writes, "Do not be conformed to *this world*, but be transformed by the renewing of your mind." However, his purpose is not to set up an ontological distinction. His purpose is merely pragmatic, to awaken the reader to habits and ideologies that are present in the world but should be rejected by Christians. But even for Paul, the church is not ethereal. The church exists in the world and exists for the sake of the world. Just a few chapters earlier, Paul writes, "For the creation (i.e., the world) waits in eager expectation for the children of God to be revealed . . . the creation itself will be liberated from its bondage to decay and brought into the freedom and glory of the children of God" (Rom 8:19–21). Because the church, even as the church, exists in the world, the distinction between the church and the world should at least be perforated in our imagination. The church swims in the same epistemic waters as everyone else. The church is part of, not above, the culture in which it is situated. This situatedness is not a bad thing. Indeed, God has chosen to be situated in human experience. But it does mean that when Christians articulate and discern theological positions and values, they do so within the culture of which they are part, using the same symbols and values.

Culture, according to Clifford Geertz, "denotes an historically transmitted pattern of meanings embodied in symbols, a system of inherited conceptions expressed in symbolic forms, by means of which men [*sic*] communicate, perpetuate, and develop their knowledge about and attitudes toward life."[28] We exist, both church and "world," within the same system of symbolic conception. So even the most "spiritual" church in Western culture still has a "secular" symbolic form. Secularity is our thought-world.

The premium that the church has placed on its own institutional survival, the need for innovation, the perceivable omission of prayer and sacrament from so many denominational and educational strategies for ecclesial "vitality," the overall desire to have something to show for our efforts, and our default obsession with our own activity are evidence that we in the church are just as secular as everyone else. Think again about the pastoral job descriptions we mentioned earlier and the disproportionate stock invested in organizational leadership over prayer and spiritual depth. James K. A. Smith clarifies, in case anyone was mistaken, "We now inhabit this self-sufficient immanent order, *even if we believe in transcendence.*"[29] To repeat Taylor, "faith, even for the staunchest believer, is one human possibility among others."[30] Even though we are tempted to think secularization is outside the church, there's no binary wherein the church gets to be spiritual or sacred, while the world outside is secular. If we are inclined to believe, with Rob Bell, that everything is spiritual, we must also confess that everything is secular.[31]

Even prayer eludes us, as so many of the members of my own church have attested. Prayer has become just one human activity among others and not a very efficient one, at that. We can list prayer on our agendas alongside taking out the trash and folding the laundry. Churches can place it on the calendar as a service or an activity before or after a board meeting. We are all secular. Christians and churches are no exception. The real question is will we be secular in such a way that we remain "open to something beyond," or will we remain closed and buffered from the transcendent?[32] How must we inhabit this secular age, and can we still pray within it?

IT'S DIFFICULT BECAUSE IT'S SOFT

According to John Swinton, "In an 'age of science,' spiritual care has come to be regarded as a form of 'soft knowledge.'"[33] In the immanent frame, the empiricist regime, the question of meaning becomes a secondary question, subordinate to explanation and practical use. This is why we don't teach philosophy to first graders. This rationality would like to do without pesky questions about the meaning of love, and grief, and beauty, and life. It would rather account for life's meaning in more quantifiable and nomothetic terms. It would "like to do without ontological claims altogether and just make do with moral reactions. . . . People of this bent would like to declare this issue of meaning a pseudo-question and brand the various frameworks within which it finds an answer as gratuitous inventions."[34] Indeed, for example, this is why psychology exists. When the speculative, soft sciences, like philosophy and theology, lost their epistemic authority to the "objective" advantage of "hard" sciences, we still needed some way of answering the questions that were once addressed by philosophers, theologians, and poets. We may have had a new understanding of what accounted for "truth," but our questions hadn't really changed. We still wanted to know what love meant. We still wanted to know the meaning of life. And if these were to be more than pseudo-questions, we needed a scientifically serious way of addressing them. So, in the newly formed power vacuum of modern knowledge, psychology was born, promising to give objective, verifiable, demonstrable, and "scientific" answers to the questions that once belonged in the purview of the so-called soft sciences.

Prayer, then, becomes merely a human behavior. The pseudo-question of God's action on the other end (*pseudo-* because it cannot be falsified, verified, or replicated) becomes reduced to fodder for speculation. So the only meaningful way of discussing prayer in a secular age is to discuss its effects on the pray-er—the psychological, spiritual, and biological effects.[35] Prayer is a health benefit, and that's why we'll put up with the possibility that it may also be a theological and mystical reality. The question of what God is up to—the God whose very existence, let alone *action*, is contested, at best—is more or less off the table.

What has happened in the immanent frame is essentially what Andrew Root and others have deemed "the epistemic fallacy." According to Root, "The epistemic fallacy is the belief that human knowers construct reality through their epistemological operations."[36] The double-conflation of reality with human reason (upward conflation) and reality itself with socialization and immanence (downward conflation) leaves human beings in an existential crisis. We are the top dog of a reality that doesn't have any point of reference outside itself. Ontology—reality itself—is reduced to epistemology—what we can know, use, prove, and replicate. Therefore, there's no point in exerting energy speculating or thinking about what a God who may or may not even exist is doing. Theological knowledge is hardly to be considered knowledge at all. We can't "know" the transcendent side of prayer, so let's just look at what human beings are doing and whether or not they're benefiting from it.

In response to this double conflation, modern theologians have tried various ways of redeeming the validity of theological knowledge and the importance of prayer. For example, Fredrick Schleiermacher worked hard to substantiate the legitimacy of theology on account of its usefulness to the church. He described prayer less as a genuine interaction between God and people and more as "a means of allaying our disquietude."[37] Categories of "religion," "discipleship," and "faithfulness" have been subtly replaced by the more generic and innocuous concept of "spirituality." While religion is often closely related in people's minds to institutional authority, corruption, and hegemonic monotheistic persuasions, the term *spirituality* is still yet palatable.[38] We are okay with looking at the concrete therapeutic effects of the abstract concept of spirituality. We still encourage "mindfulness," yoga classes, and meditation because they have use to us; they do not require any overt reference to a transcendent other or deity, and they are not dogmatic or doctrinal. The secular age can still tolerate transcendence and embrace a vague spirituality without a theistic referent because its utilities, the part that "makes a difference," are immanent.

"For those who pray," writes David Auten in his memoir, "it is quite natural to wonder where the line is between the voice in your own head and that 'other' voice. Actual prayer is dynamic, and what you find yourself saying or hearing in prayer is never a matter of absolute clarity or certainty. That's what makes faith, faith. Spontaneity and surprise, the sublime and the subliminal, are indelible marks of this mystical terrain."[39] The secular age directs our attention to effectiveness, practicality, and utility—away from the "sublime and the subliminal"—so even devout Christians with serious doctrinal commitments and religious affiliations will gravitate to the instrumental valuation of their spirituality and their prayer life. But what happens when prayer doesn't get "results"? What happens when prayer does not produce outcomes or contribute to our development? What's its value then? We get frustrated, confused, and we feel guilty: "I must be doing something wrong." The reason that prayer becomes a source of frustration for so many of us, including pastors and priests, is because prayer is a "soft science" in an empiricist regime of knowledge.

KNOWING VERSUS KNOWING

According to David Hay, "Spiritual or religious knowing is very different from knowledge of factual information, or speculation about religion. It is much more like a direct sensory awareness."[40] As bounded and buffered selves in the immanent frame, we have a certain comfortability with factual information. We like things that are both measurable and useful to us, things that serve our development. We like ideas that we can control or observe from an objective point of view. However, when we pray, we do not address an object that we can control. As Stanley Grenz puts it, "In prayer, we address the God who is willing and able to act."[41] We address (and are addressed by) a person, not an idea. And persons are unknowable in the modern sense of the word—and frustratingly so. Persons are inherently distinct and therefore mysterious. We can never do without distinctiveness in personal relationships. In the I-Thou relationship, there is never a point at which the other is possessed or attained by the self. Once attained, in this sense, the other would cease to be an "other"; it would become a dead thing at the disposal of the self. Relational knowledge upholds the uncontrollability of the other and the *integrity* (for lack of a better term) of the personhood of the other. Relational knowledge is less like the apprehension of information and more like an embrace.

Modernity doesn't really allow for relational knowledge because it assumes that the ability to be known is inherent to all existence.[42] In his important work *Exclusion and Embrace*, Miroslav Volf offers a phenomenology of embrace, a "free and mutual giving and receiving"—something we might well relate to what we've already discussed as *resonance* or *abiding*—an uncontrollable connection that cannot be forced or engineered.[43] Volf explains that true embrace is not a "bear hug": "The embrace itself depends on the success in resisting the vortex of de-differentiation through active or passive assimilation, yet without retreating into self-insulation."[44] Volf goes on to cite the Israeli cultural anthropologist Zali D. Gurevitch, whose claim to fame comes from his creative conceptualization of "the third body," which is the shared experience, mutual understanding, and unique relationship that emerges when two individuals communicate. Gurevitch argues against the notion that all unknowing should eventually lead to knowing—that is, the basic epistemological presumption of modernity.[45] Volf's explanation of this "ability-not-to-understand" is helpful. He writes, "The initial 'inability to understand' may be tacitly predicated on the desire to understand the other on the self's own terms, within the framework of its own reflexivity, whereas the other may not be understandable within the self's framework precisely on account of being the other."[46] When we encounter God, we need to become comfortable with the very uncomfortable notion of "not-understanding." To truly *know* God, to find resonance with God, and to abide in God, we need to "acquire the unusual ability *not* to understand the other."[47] We need to have the ability to *not* understand God. This ability of inability is essential to receiving prayer and abiding in *amen*.

It may be an exercise in semantics (though I would argue it is a meaningful one) to think in terms of an "ability of inability" or an "ability not to understand." In thinking about what it means to abide, perhaps what we're really talking about here is a different sort of knowledge altogether—not the sort of knowledge that possesses and disposes of objects but knowledge that preserves the otherness of the person and seeks a deep resonance rather than control. What we need to recover is what Moltmann refers to as the "desire to know in order to participate."[48]

As John Calvin puts it, "We ought not to rack our brains about God; but rather, we should contemplate him [*sic*] in his works . . . we are called to a knowledge of God: not that knowledge which, content with empty speculation, merely flits in the brain, but that which will be sound and fruitful if we duly perceive it, and if it takes root in the heart."[49] This "communicative," participatory, or "meditative" kind of knowledge is relational and oriented toward subjects rather than objects.[50] And it is only within this kind of knowledge that prayer can be properly understood.

Prayer itself is communicative—it is communication. Prayer is participatory. It relies on the initiative of a transcendent God. Prayer is meditative. It does not seek to manipulate but to indwell and to abide. Prayer is relational. It does not prioritize the outcome of our relationship with God over the relationship itself. Our default epistemology in the immanent frame doesn't have a broad enough horizon to allow for prayer. It turns everything into a utility, a measurable instrument for measurable goals. It turns prayer into a tool. But prayer is more like a song than a hammer. It bears a stronger resemblance to dancing or swinging on the trapeze than it does to building a house.

Prayer is a matter of relationship; it is not a matter of fact. It isn't something we have to "get right." According to Andrew Purves, "We are not right . . . Because Christians understand truth specifically in terms of the *name*—that is, the *person*—of Jesus, truth is about a person and a relationship which he has established from his [*sic*] side."[51] So when we pray, we are not entering into a laboratory; we are not testing God, and we are not being tested to see if we will succeed or fail. We are, rather, invited and welcomed into a loving and authentic exchange, into an abiding, with a living God who always moves toward us before we even have the thought to move.

Abiding in Relationship

Set aside everything you think you *know* about prayer—everything you've been taught about saying the right words, asking in the right way, needing to "get it right." Instead, imagine prayer as an invitation to sit with a friend, a friend who loves you before you even speak, who knows the deepest parts of you and welcomes your presence, no matter what you bring.

Prayer, in its truest form, is not about understanding a set of theological facts. It's not about mentally grasping doctrines or being able to recite the right creed. It's about abiding—an ongoing, living connection with the God who has already reached out to you. Before you say a word, God is present. Before you form a thought, God has already moved toward you in love.

Here's a step-by-step guide to practicing relational prayer:

1. *Prepare Your Space*
   Find a quiet place where you can be still. It could be a chair, a corner of a room, or even outside under the open sky. Eliminate distractions as best as you can and allow yourself to settle into this space. Bring a sense of openness with you, as if you're about to meet with someone who already knows and loves you deeply.
2. *Become Aware of Your Breathing*
   Start by focusing on your breath. Inhale slowly, feeling the air fill your lungs, and exhale even more slowly. As you breathe, imagine each breath as a reminder of God's Spirit, always with you, always sustaining you. Don't rush this. Take time to simply notice your breathing, letting it draw you into a place of awareness and stillness. Something about simply focusing on breathing can help us feel closer to God. As one of my former pastors, David Auten, used to say, "I've never felt *further* from God after focusing on my breathing."

3. *Acknowledge God's Presence*
   Before you speak or think, pause and recognize that God is already here with you. You don't have to reach for God. God has already reached for you. In this moment, you are not beginning something; you are entering into a relationship that already exists. Rest in that awareness.
4. *Release the Need for Words*
   If you feel the need to speak or write something down, go ahead—but there is no pressure to do so. You don't need to say anything formal or find the right words. Prayer in this practice is not about verbalizing perfect thoughts. It's about being with God. Let silence be okay. In fact, let it be part of your prayer. If thoughts come, acknowledge them and gently let them pass like clouds in the sky. The focus is on being in God's presence.
5. *Listen with Your Heart*
   Spend some time in this stillness, just listening. Not necessarily for an audible voice but for the quiet stirrings in your heart. Pay attention to how you feel in this moment—whether peaceful, restless, joyful, or uncertain. Know that every feeling is welcomed here and you are safe to bring your full self into this space. You don't have to fix anything or force anything to happen. You are simply abiding in a loving relationship.
6. *Respond Authentically*
   If words come naturally—whether of gratitude, worry, joy, or grief—let them rise without censoring yourself. Speak to God as you would to a close friend. Know that God delights in hearing from you, not because your words need to be perfect but because God delights in you. If no words come, let that be okay too. Your presence is enough.
7. *Rest in God's Love*
   Before you close your time of prayer, take a moment to simply rest. Feel the truth of God's love for you, right now, just as you are. Imagine God holding you, moving toward you, long

before you even thought of praying. Let that truth sink into your heart. You are not here to "get it right"—you are here to be in relationship.

8. *Close Gently*

   When you're ready to end this time of prayer, don't rush. Slowly bring your attention back to your surroundings but carry with you the sense of abiding in God's presence. As you go back to your daily tasks, remind yourself that this relationship continues. God is still with you, still moving toward you in love.

This prayer practice is not about achieving something or performing in a particular way. It's about dwelling in a relationship that already exists, a loving and authentic exchange with a living God who is always moving toward you. There's nothing you have to prove or perfect here. Just come and be.

Amen.

CHAPTER THREE

Haunted by Transcendence

The fields of psychology and psychoanalysis came of age during the early to mid-twentieth century. The aforementioned shift from the ideographic to the nomothetic—from mystery to the immanent frame—had left an epistemic power vacuum. However, while authority shifted away from "soft sciences" like philosophy and theology, and toward biology and instrumental reason, people were still interested in understanding the meaning of life and the deeper questions of love, purpose, and existence—questions that had once been answered by philosophers, poets, and theologians. The questions lingered, even as our trust in the disciplines that once addressed those questions waned. Some thinkers, such as B. F. Skinner, the father of behaviorism, tried to double down and skirt those questions. Skinner believed that all human actions could be understood through observable behaviors rather than internal mental states, which he saw as irrelevant or difficult to study scientifically.

Charles Taylor helpfully criticized behaviorism, particularly its reductionist approach to understanding human behavior. In his influential work *The Explanation of Behaviour*, Taylor argued that behaviorism, which focuses solely on observable behavior and external stimuli, is insufficient for explaining the complexity of human action.[1] While Skinner's determinist and immanent view represents a historical extreme that has generally been rejected as a reductionist perspective, the basic operating epistemology persists and occasionally rears its head in other forms, such as biological determinism and scientific positivism. In the early years of the twentieth century, however, appetites were still whet for some discipline to address these questions. People had questions for "soft" sciences but we were only satisfied with "hard" sciences. Enter psychology.

Psychology was born in the power vacuum of epistemology, promising hard answers to the questions that were once addressed by the soft sciences. Instead of poets and philosophers, we'd have psychoanalysts. Instead of theologians, we'd have psychologists. Psychology, we hoped, would give us the answers that theology could not. The immanent frame would solve the puzzle and eradicate the mystery.

Psychology has experienced a lot of change since those early days and, in large part, has come to understand itself in a more hermeneutical light.[2] In any case, however, that early promise has not been kept. Psychology has not saved us from being haunted by transcendence. Even in the mist of psychology's coming of age, thinkers were cross-pressured by the desire for demonstrable, replicable, and verifiable knowledge and the inevitability of the irreplicable, mysterious, and transcendent. According to James K. A. Smith, "We live in the twilight of both gods and idols. But their ghosts have refused to depart, and every once in a while we might be surprised to find ourselves tempted by belief, by intimations of transcendence."[3]

HENRI AND ERIK: A PARABLE OF CROSS-PRESSURE

The lives of two renowned twentieth-century scholars illustrate well the cross-pressure of our secular age, as well as the epistemic difficulty of prayer. Henri Nouwen and Erik Erikson were promising young scholars who shared a common interest but whose life paths diverged from one another. Erikson was about a generation older than Nouwen, but had they been the same age, one could imagine that they might have been friends. The ways in which they navigated the pressures of immanence and transcendence may be instructive for us, especially as we consider our own posture toward prayer. We must realize that neither Nouwen nor Erikson can be said to have gotten it right, but I think their stories resonate with the story of modernity on an atomic level.

Nouwen, born in 1932 in the Netherlands, was raised in a devout Catholic family, where faith and church life played a central role from a young age. According to Michael O'Laughlin, even Henri's playtime fantasies centered on religiosity. He convinced his parents to let him set up a "miniature chapel in the attic," where he would dress in priestly vestments made for him by his grandmother and "say Mass with a paten, chalice, and other liturgical accessories."[4] His upbringing was marked by a deep spiritual formation, which influenced his lifelong focus on pastoral care, contemplative spirituality, and community. As a Dutchman raised in an "enterprising" culture, Nouwen always felt pressure to achieve and maintain status.[5] But when it came time to discern his career path, he followed his dream and entered the priesthood.

Nouwen was a good student and quickly became fascinated by theology. He was charmed by Søren Kierkegaard's work, in particular. Kierkegaard's existential and theological insights resonated with many themes Nouwen would later explore, such as the nature of faith, the human condition, vulnerability, and the journey of the self. Kierkegaard's idea that despair is part of becoming oneself and recognizing one's dependence on God resonated with Nouwen's early awareness of existential and spiritual struggles and may have ultimately shaped his understanding of suffering as a pathway to intimacy with God. Even though he had nurturing parents and a loving family, Nouwen was plagued throughout his life by a sense of loneliness.[6] As Michael Higgins and Kevin Burns put it, "This was the society Nouwen grew up in: clearly delineated boundaries, tribal independence, and fervently protected spheres."[7] Nouwen chafed under these conditions. He was much more of a free spirit than such a world allowed. He felt restless, and according to Michael Ford, "the practice of prayer was never easy for Henri."[8] He struggled with his sense of identity and longed to understand who he was and why he existed.

Nouwen was plagued by the thought that he needed a purpose, a higher calling, and he needed a barometer to measure his success. For this, he looked to his father: "His own inner uncertainties became tangled, very early on in life, with a sense that he could never measure up to his father's expectations."[9] Perhaps driven by these feelings, the young Nouwen felt the need to further legitimize himself. In the epistemic power vacuum of the secular age, "theories of an unconscious self, of the inalienable sexuality of human beings, of multiple centers of personality—such as the ego, the superego and the id—and many other progressive and unsettling ideas were in the air."[10] As Michael Ford puts it, "Psychotherapy was already replacing spiritual and moral guidance as the primary method for relieving mental and emotional disorders, while psychologists and psychiatrists were increasingly viewed as 'the new priesthood.'"[11] In this changing epistemological ecosystem, Nouwen wasn't satisfied with the priesthood alone. He also wanted to become a psychoanalyst: "Pathologies, research samples, statistics, schemas of personality development, and care studies now formed important new fields of reference for him."[12] Perhaps he'd found his barometer.

Erikson, born in 1902 in Germany, had a complex upbringing. He was raised by his Jewish mother and stepfather, who concealed the truth about his biological father for much of his childhood. This sense of identity confusion, coupled with his outsider status as a Jewish child in a predominantly Lutheran society, deeply informed his later work on identity formation and psychosocial development. Erikson's mother, Karla, was a free spirit herself and brilliant in her own right. Karla was dedicated to her Jewish faith and customs but also had a deep appreciation of the work of Søren Kierkegaard for his very Danish, but also very Christian, "appeal."[13] From a young age, Erik would have been exposed to Kierkegaard's Christian existentialism, and one can only speculate how and if Erikson and Nouwen may have bonded over their shared interest and the shared influence of the free thinking and idiographic imagination that would have shaped both of their childhoods. Karla was an artist and took great interest in "unconventional artists and craftspeople."[14] Erik's German society was rigid, like Nouwen's, but his mother's influence created in him a deep fascination for the unresolvable mysteries of life.[15]

Erik had a strong bond with his mother in his early years of childhood. When Karla fell in love with Erik's pediatrician, Theodore Homburger, a short man with a goatee, it could have been interpreted as an intrusion.[16] On Erik's third birthday, Karla and Theodore were married. From that day on, Erik was told that Theodore was his biological father, even though it took several more years for Erik to be given the name Homburger. It also must have been suspicious that, years later, Theodore legally adopted Erik, which would hardly have been necessary unless Theodore was not, in fact, his father. Of course, he wasn't. In fact, Erik's father's identity remains unknown. Nevertheless, although there were tensions between them, Theodore was a loving, if somewhat strict, father to Erik.

Something in Erikson's subconscious, however, must have known all along that he did not really belong to Theodore. He later recounted the feeling of "doubt" in his identity, in his words, "all through my childhood years."[17] In contrast to his mother, Theodore had no regard for Erikson's artistic interests and from early on urged him toward a career that would make him some money and earn him some status.[18] Theodore wanted him to become a doctor, like himself. Erikson did the next best thing. He became a student of psychology, hardly as "hard" a science as Theodore may have preferred, but at least it wasn't art. Despite not even knowing all that well who Sigmund Freud was, Erikson's potential as a psychoanalyst was obvious. Anna Freud saw Erikson's potential and recruited him to study in Vienna.

Nouwen also became a student in psychology. In 1957, the same year that he was ordained as a Catholic priest, he became a doctoral student at the Catholic University of Nijmegan.[19] In the early 1960s, he moved to the United States to study at the Menninger Clinic in Kansas, a prestigious institution known for its work in psychiatry and psychoanalysis. It was during this time, in the mid-1960s, that Nouwen delved deeply into psychology, working with notable figures in the field and seeking to integrate his theological background with psychoanalytic insights: "Clinical psychology attempts to bring scientific rigor to the study of human nature."[20] Nouwen saw in psychoanalysis a kind of credibility that could substantiate his thinking and, perhaps more importantly, substantiate him as a thinker and teacher.

While it would have benefited him professionally to stay grounded in the more nomothetic frames of reference that were in the air of the epistemic landscape of the field dominated by Freudian sensibility, Nouwen couldn't quite cut it as a "hard" scientist. He wasn't keen to submit to what he began to see as reductions and dependencies that were inadequate for addressing the deeper spiritual and transcendent questions of his Catholic persuasion. The psychological frameworks that Nouwen was learning were not fully compatible with his theological proclivities and search for meaning. Nouwen, who was navigating his identity and calling, was challenged by the apparent rigidity of psychology and struggled to integrate his own commitments, including Kierkegaard's idea of the will to be oneself, into his understanding of the more "scientific" world of psychoanalysis. "No immediate synthesis was possible," writes Michael O'Laughlin, "between the quite divergent value systems of Catholicism and psychological theory when Nouwen was a student."[21]

Henri was cross-pressured by the immanent and the transcendent. He discovered that clinical psychology was often too reductive—too dependent on testing, statistical models, systems of verifiability and replication. It was, to Nouwen, too cold and detached to get to the thing that mattered to him. His dissatisfaction grew as he realized that psychoanalysis lacked the depth to address the spiritual and existential questions that were central to his life and ministry. Nouwen was looking for more than what psychology could offer. He sought to understand the human person in relation to God, mystery, and transcendence and felt that psychology's empirical methods left these dimensions unexplored. According to O'Loughlin, "To become a psychological or medical professional involves taking on the serious demeanor and detachment that we all expect from someone with scientific training . . . Each step he took toward becoming a psychologist may have seemed to be taking him farther and farther away from the ideals of the gospel."[22] When Nouwen discovered phenomenology and the writings of Edmund Husserl, he must have felt relieved. He became deeply interested in the more phenomenological approach, of which the motto is "'go back to the thing itself'—as a summons to retrieve, relive, the original experience."[23] Nevertheless, he had hit a wall.

Nouwen chose as the topic for his doctoral thesis the work of Anton Boisen, the American who created clinical pastoral education in seminaries. According to O'Laughlin, "Nouwen's thesis on Boisen, when presented in Nijmegen University, was not immediately approved. Henri was told that if it were to be accepted, he would have to recast the thesis as a more scientific work based on statistics and clinical models. Henri balked at this attempt to 'straightjacket' him into a narrow professionalism. He determined to drop the ill-fated thesis and leave Nijmegen with a *doctorandus* degree. The *doctorandus* is Holland is a professional qualification, while the doctoral is an academic, research degree."[24]

After seven years of doctoral work, Nouwen got what basically amounts to the equivalent of a master's degree. This, of course, is nothing to scoff at, but it was hardly what he had set out to do. He didn't make it as a psychoanalyst. Oh, how different the world may have been had he made it. Nouwen departed from the field of psychology, electing to let the questions of transcendence remain appropriately mysterious rather than reducing them to instrumental numbers and figures. He devoted his life to the ideographic work of listening to the Holy Spirit, the life of prayer.

Erik's journey was different. Rather than feeling crushed under the rubrics of scientific rationality, Erikson thrived. In 1933, he became a full member of the Vienna Psychoanalytic Society. According to Lawrence Friedman, "[Erik's] formal training in Vienna gave him a comparatively clear and coherent system of thought and an explicit theoretical framework for clinical observation."[25] He was natural and budding psychoanalyst in his own right. But, like Nouwen, Erikson was "haunted by transcendence."[26] Even as a star student of psychology in the Freudian school with its presumed positivism—a hypothesis that there were "universals" beneath the layers of human diversity—Erikson remained influenced by existentialist and poetic thinkers like Kierkegaard, Nietzsche, Goethe, and Blake. Even as he was deepening himself in the wells of Freudian psychoanalytical epistemology, Erikson was enthralled by the mysterious things that evaded structural analysis and could not be contained in "universals."[27]

Erikson went on to take a deep interest in ethnography and sociology. It was at Harvard that Erik met anthropologists like Margaret Mead, Gregory Bateson, and Scudder Mekeel. These influences led him to Yale, where he began his own quests in sociology. At the urging of his friends from Harvard, he went from Yale to an unlikely place—the Pine Ridge Reservation in South Dakota, with the *Oceti Sakowin*, the people of the Sioux Nation.[28] He began a journey out of the clinic and the laboratory and into the situated knowledge of ethnography.

By the mid-1970s, Nouwen had fully transitioned from psychoanalysis and began to focus on pastoral care, spirituality, and theology. Still informed by many of the insights of psychology, he seems to have made a conscious decision to enter deeply into the transcendent. His teaching and writing during this period reflect his growing emphasis on Christian mysticism and the spiritual journey, culminating in works like *The Wounded Healer*, where he offered a vision of ministry that embraced human vulnerability and divine mystery.[29] This period marked his emergence as a leading voice in spiritual theology, a role he would carry for the rest of his life. Nouwen's journey during these decades laid the groundwork for his later, more contemplative works, such as *The Return of the Prodigal Son*, which captured his ultimate commitment to the integration of spiritual life, pastoral care, and the embrace of mystery that psychoanalysis, for all its insights, could not provide.[30]

THE EVERYMAN AND THE SELF-MADE MAN

One can see how Erikson and Nouwen may have liked each other. They certainly could have resonated with each other's insecurities. They were both stuck between transcendence and immanence, and consequently neither was completely at home in his field or in his skin. I suspect that many of us can relate to this. I know more than one pastor who would admit (maybe after a couple of beers) that they, too, struggle with the haunting suspicion that all the gooey stuff of transcendence—all the *pointless* things they get paid to do—like prayer and the sacraments, are overshadowed by the pressing need to grow the church and balance the budget. (Okay, maybe it doesn't take a couple of beers.) Perhaps this is why "leadership" has become a little more comfortable to talk about than "ministry." Pastors, more and more, are seeing themselves as leaders, entrepreneurs, innovators, and directors as opposed to *ministers* of Word and sacrament. Leadership, I can understand. Ministry is just too fuzzy. If pastors feel this, then so must the people sitting in the pews. Ministry is usurped by management. The *pastoral* is supplanted by the administrative. The priesthood of all believers is traded for membership on the church council.

One might stop me here to ask, "Is the tension between the scientific (or positivist) and the ideographic really analogous to the immanent and the transcendent? Isn't the difference between praying and balancing the budget a little different than the difference between ethnography and psychology?" Of course, there are indeed differences. But I suggest that the principles that cause these tensions are the same, all constructed on the scaffolding of modernity's immanent frame. The tension between psychology and ethnography mirrors the dynamics between prayer and management because *both* pairs reflect a broader conflict rooted in modernity and secularization. Psychology and management align with modernity's emphasis on measurement, control, and predictability, seeking to categorize and manage human behavior. Ethnography and prayer, on the other hand, emphasize presence, relationality, and the unpredictability of lived experiences. This creates a clash where secular, rational approaches attempt to systematize and control what is inherently relational, mysterious, and beyond full human understanding. Both tensions highlight the struggle between the desire for control and the acceptance of the unknown.

According to Charles Taylor, "There always have been a great many people who have been cross-pressured between two basic orientations; who want to respect as much as they can the 'scientific' shape of the imminent order, as they have been led to see it; or who fear the effect of religious 'fanaticism'; still cannot help believing that there is something more than the merely imminent."[31] Nouwen and Erikson were both products of modernity, just like you and me. Both bared in themselves the tension between puzzle and mystery, immanent and transcendent. But both men, in their own way, reached a crossroads in the cross-pressure.

Erik saw himself as a self-made man, nowhere more strongly symbolized than in his own renaming of himself from Homburger to Erikson—a father to himself. By 1944, Erikson had pretty much lost interest in the Freudian psychological school in which he'd thrived when he was in Vienna. He wasn't working in the clinic but in the field. He had all but abandoned any vocational connection to the stewardship of developmental theory. That is, until the birth of his son Neil.

Erik's wife, Joan, was forty-one years old when Neil was born. Unlike her previous births, this one was problematic. Due to the geriatric nature of her pregnancy, she had to be put under heavy sedation, and when she awoke in a daze, she wanted to hold her new child. She asked the nurses where Neil was, but the hospital staff avoided telling her. Eventually, after a frustrating and confusing delay, the obstetrician told Joan that her baby had some serious problems and was being cared for elsewhere. While Joan had still been under sedation, a few other doctors on the hospital staff summoned Erik to tell him that his child, Neil, had Down syndrome. They explained that the child would never be able to hold up his head and wouldn't live more than a year or so. According to Friedman, "They recommended immediate institutionalization," and that is what Erik decided to do after consulting his friend Margaret Mead (who had no documented expertise in Down syndrome research, unlike another friend, Dr. Spock, whose knowledge was cutting edge).[32] Before Joan even had a chance to see her child, Neil's fate was sealed. He was sent to an institution to live separated and alienated from the rest of his family.

Neil's birth threw the Erikson family into turmoil. Joan and Erik felt "numbness and disbelief that they had not created a healthy child."[33] Erik, who'd been lied to for his entire childhood about the identity of his father, chose to carry on the tradition and lie to his other children about their sibling. He told them that their brother had died in childbirth. In fact, Neil would live for twenty-two years in an institution, receiving only occasional visits from his mother and even fewer visits from his father.

Out of this trauma, Erikson was energized to pick up where he left off years earlier, when he was thriving in the safety of the theoretical world of the clinic and the classroom in Vienna. Erikson dealt with the trauma of his son's birth (much of which was created by his own, chosen response) by essentially locking himself in his cottage and writing *Childhood and Society*, the work that gifted the world with the "eight stages of development" that continue to be so instructive—a multitude of critiques notwithstanding—for everyone from pediatricians to youth pastors. During this tense time in the Erikson family, Erik sought refuge in the controllability of scientific rationality. Joan became a partner in his writing, and according to Friedman, "the Eriksons acknowledged they were fashioning a developmental framework for health and normalcy" in contrast to their "unfinished" and "incomplete" child, the "victim of a delayed physical and mental development."[34] In fact, Neil was more a victim of *abandonment* than of any kind of "delay." According to Friedman, working on developmental psychology "helped to assure them [the Eriksons] that they were developmentally healthy even as Neil, located elsewhere, was not. In effect, Erik and Joan had an emotional stake in placing Neil at the fringe of their map just as he remained distant from their family."[35]

Erikson, the self-made man, found solace in self-creating a picture of developmental health and normalcy. He found his own peace, not in the transcendent—that was far too chaotic—but in the immanent, the controllable (or, at least, the illusion thereof). Even though he would later lament how practitioners adopted his work as a fixed and hierarchical schema, what Erikson gave us in his eight stages was a tidy narrative that strategically excluded Neil and those who transcend the structured frame of developmentalism. One wonders what Erikson might have done if he had made a different decision when Neil was born. What would his life have been like if he had embraced the uncontrollability of his situation, if he had embraced Neil?

Nouwen, on the other hand, had cut his teeth and become one of the premier pastoral theologians of his time, holding positions at Harvard and Yale—not unlike Erikson before him. But he reached a breaking point. In his book *In the Name of Jesus*, Nouwen writes, "After twenty years in the academic world as a teacher of pastoral psychology, pastoral theology, and Christian spirituality, I began to experience a deep inner threat."[36] He became so preoccupied with his more clinical and academic absorptions that he was burning out. His longing for peace had caught up with his striving for excellence: "After twenty-five years of priesthood, I found myself praying poorly, living somewhat isolated from other people, and very much preoccupied with burning issues. Everyone was saying that I was doing really well, but something inside was telling me that my success was putting my own soul in danger."[37] Nouwen made the decision to leave the academy, leave his prestigious position and title, and become an "Everyman," an assistant at L'Arche.[38]

L'Arche is an international federation of communities where people with and without intellectual disabilities live and work together. Each L'Arche community typically consists of homes where people with intellectual disabilities (referred to as "core members") live alongside staff (often called "assistants"), who help provide support and care. Nouwen left the cushy prestige of an Ivy League professorship to fold laundry with people who had never read any of his books. Of course, there is a degree of condescension that we must check in describing the contrast between academia and living with people with disabilities as a step down, but even recognizing the dignity and beauty of working in L'Arche, the contrast is observable.[39]

Nouwen writes,

> So I moved from Harvard to L'Arche, from the best and brightest, wanting to rule the world, to men and women who had few or no words and were considered, at best, marginal to the needs of our society. It was a very hard and painful move . . . After twenty years of being free to go where I wanted and to discuss what I chose, the small, hidden life with people whose broken minds and bodies demand a strict daily routine in which words are the least requirement does not immediately appear as the solution for spiritual burnout. And yet, my new life at L'Arche is offering me new words to use in speaking about Christian leadership in the future because I have found there all the challenges that we are facing as ministers of God's Word.[40]

Nouwen was comfortable in the confines of his very good work in the classroom and the study, but the demands of immanence—academic productivity, pedagogical performance, mastery of his discipline—were crushing to him. The cross-pressure broke Nouwen, and he sought his peace in the uncontrollability of human life, in the simple immersion into friendship as an end in itself: "For Nouwen, the gospel was becoming not just a message explaining how God long ago brought into being a new spiritual reality through Jesus; he was also coming to see it as a blueprint for how we might live our lives and find God today."[41] Nouwen retreated into the transcendence of simply being with and for others, specifically people with disabilities.

"Nouwen was not a saintly figure," writes O'Loughlin. "Instead, Nouwen was one of us . . . Nouwen once suggested that his middle initials, 'J. M.,' stood for 'just me.' . . . He lived his life as an Everyman."[42] Nouwen found himself in relationship and in prayer, as best he could. But one may be permitted to ask, "Why couldn't Nouwen maintain his spirituality within the immanent?" Many of us don't have a choice. We can't run to a monastery or to L'Arche. Most of us can't up and leave our context and escape into transcendence. It's an open question whether Nouwen really was an "everyman" and what may have happened to him had he done what most of us have to do—continue in the struggle, in the cross-pressure and the malaise of modernity.

Erikson and Nouwen were similar in many ways. They both loved Kierkegaard; they both had a fascination with psychology and a haunting interest in the mysterious and the artistic. But the paths they chose, and the epistemologies in which they found their peace, led them in divergent directions. Erikson held, like a life preserver, onto the knowledge of the clinic, while Nouwen struggled to grasp "the knowledge gained in prayer that God loved and accepted him just as he was."[43]

Born thirty years apart, Erik Erikson and Henri Nouwen both represent the kind of cross-pressure that is pervasively characteristic of the secular age in which we live. They both reached a similar crossroads. Must we resolve the mysteries of life? Can we order the disorder? Can we solve the puzzle of meaning? Or might we embrace the imprecision of human knowledge, accept the uncontrollability of the world, and simply *be* and participate in the mystery, embracing without resolving?

I'm not sure either man could have told you before their deaths that they found resolution. I suspect the cross-pressure, the haunting of immanence and transcendence, stuck with them. There is no indication in any of Nouwen's writing that prayer ever became "easy" for him. In fact, his works are chock-full of confessions about prayer's illusiveness in his life. I put these two in contrast not to show one as a heel and one as a hero but to offer a picture of two conflicted individuals with whom I think we can resonate.

THE MAGNETIC FORCE OF BELIEF AND DISBELIEF

We are all caught in the "nova effect" of the secular age, caught between the "self-made man" (modernity's man) and the "everyman," caught between belief and unbelief.[44] Charles Taylor says that the *fragilization* of belief is a two-way fragilization.[45] If you are someone who believes, you can't help but have moments when your belief is contested, when you need concrete data, and you just don't trust your experience of God. You're going to have a moment when you think, "Ugh, is this true? Or is this just about the family I grew up in? No, no, no, I believe it, I believe it, I believe it." Like Nouwen, you will have moments when your belief is challenged by the malaise of institutional acceleration, and you may feel the need to retreat into the monastery, the sanctuary, or your own version of what the L'Arche community was for Henri.

But this goes both ways. On the flip side, every doubter will be haunted by belief as well. If you're one who does not believe, you'll have moments when you'll find yourself captivated by the transcendent, by the stuff of mystery that cannot be quantified or instrumentalized. Like Erikson, you'll be challenged by the possibility of the divine, and you may find yourself retreating into the study and back to your spreadsheets and formulas to reground yourself in the safety of objectivity and certitude.

The magnetic force of belief—the transcendent and mysterious—creates, in our modern world, the need for its opposite. But, likewise, the force of disbelief—of objective and nomothetic conflation of reality with rules and formulas for optimization and development—will also create the need for its opposite. The Henri Nouwens will be haunted by doubt (you are not alone), and the Erik Eriksons will be haunted by transcendence (again, you are not alone). So we find ourselves forever caught between mystery and certainty, each pulling us toward the other, reminding us that in our deepest questioning, we are never truly alone. This tension between belief and disbelief, between mystery and certainty, points to the importance of prayer as a space where both can meet. In prayer, we hold our questions and our hopes before God, allowing our doubts to be met with presence rather than mere answers. Praying together strengthens this shared experience, reminding us that faith isn't about certainty but about journeying through life's mysteries together. In communal prayer, we find support in the paradox, each voice affirming that our searching is seen and that we are not alone in our seeking.

Abiding Under Pressure

Imagine standing at the center of two powerful forces pulling you, like magnets, in opposite directions. On one side is the pull of belief, the desire to connect with something greater, the haunting presence of the uncontrollable and the mysterious. On the other side is the tug of doubt, the sense that what's in front of us—what we can see, measure, and control—is all there is, all that's relevant. This tension, this sense of being caught between belief and unbelief, is what Charles Taylor calls "cross-pressure."

We live in a milieu that limits our view of reality to what's tangible and immediate, often sidelining the transcendent. Even those of us who are most "spiritual" are, like Henri Nouwen, conflicted and tempted by the allure of instrumental rationality, crushed under a framework where science, technology, and secular thinking dominate how we understand the world. And those of us who might otherwise desire to enter transcendence may be, like Erik Erikson, drawn to the comfort of the illusion of controllability. Even for those who believe in God, this immanent frame exerts a constant pressure. We feel drawn to prayer, maybe we even feel guilty that don't pray enough, but we're also surrounded by the persistent hum of doubt, asking, "Is there really anything real in this prayer stuff?"

This is cross-pressure—the feeling of being stretched between these two realities. It's not just an intellectual struggle but also an emotional and spiritual tension, felt deeply in our everyday lives. And while this can make prayer feel difficult or uncertain, it can also be a powerful place for honesty and perhaps even an abiding connection with God.

Here's a prayer practice that invites you to bring that tension into your conversation with God. Rather than trying to resolve it, this practice acknowledges the reality of cross-pressure and opens a space for meeting God right in the midst of it, for being spiritual even in the secular.

1. *Find a Quiet Space*
   Begin by finding a space where you can be alone with your thoughts. This space doesn't have to be sacred in any conventional sense; it can be anywhere you can reflect without

interruption—a park bench, a room in your home, or even a car. The key is to set aside some time to be present, allowing yourself to acknowledge the complexity of your internal landscape.

2. *Name the Tension*
Take a few deep breaths and start by naming the tension you feel. Do you feel caught between belief and doubt? Between the sacred and the secular? Between the desire for transcendence and the demands of everyday life? Don't rush this part. Let yourself sit with the discomfort of the cross-pressure. You don't have to solve it or make it go away—just acknowledge that it's there.

3. *Offer Your Doubts and Desires*
Now, in your mind or aloud, offer both your doubts and your desires to God. You can do this however it feels most natural to you. You might say something like, "God, I want faith, but it's hard. I feel the weight of the world's pull, and I also feel the pull toward you." Or "Lord, I believe; help my unbelief." Be honest about where you are. God invites your whole self into prayer—both the parts that long for transcendence and the parts that resist it.

4. *Invite God's Presence into the Cross-Pressure*
Once you've offered your thoughts and feelings, invite God's presence into the tension. You might say, "God, meet me in this tension, in the pull between belief and unbelief, between the immanent and the transcendent." Imagine God sitting with you in this uncomfortable space, not as a solution or a quick fix but as a comforting presence that understands both sides of the struggle.

5. *Listen in the Stillness*
Take a moment to be still. Don't rush to conclusions or expect immediate clarity. Just sit in the presence of God and listen. Sometimes God speaks in words, but often, God's presence is felt more as a quiet assurance—a sense that you are not alone, even in the midst of your doubts and questions.

If your mind starts to wander, gently bring your focus back to this moment of stillness.

6. *Embrace the Mystery*

   Rather than seeking to resolve the tension, allow yourself to embrace the mystery of it. Cross-pressure doesn't always have an easy answer. Living in the modern world means that we will often feel the pull of both belief and doubt. Indeed, as Paul Tillich insisted, faith and doubt belong to each other. Instead of trying to escape that tension, trust that God is present within it. As you pray, remind yourself that faith is not about having all the answers but about continuing the conversation, even when the path isn't clear.

7. *Thank God for the Space to Wrestle*

   As you come to the end of this prayer, take a moment to thank God for creating space for you to wrestle with these questions. You might say something like, "Thank you, God, for being present in the tension, for not needing me to have it all figured out." This is a space where you can be fully human, fully caught between belief and unbelief, and still fully loved by God.

8. *Carry the Cross-Pressure with You*

   When you finish this time of prayer, carry the awareness of cross-pressure with you. Know that the tension between the immanent and the transcendent is not something you need to escape but something you can live with. Trust that God is with you in both the sacred and the ordinary, in your moments of belief and your moments of doubt. This prayer practice doesn't promise an escape from the pressure of the immanent frame; nor does it suggest that doubt is something to be eradicated. Instead, it invites you to see the tension as part of the journey, a place where God can meet you in all your complexity. Rather than seeking to resolve the cross-pressure, this practice opens a space for you to dwell in it, knowing that God is present with you in every pull and pause.

   Amen.

CHAPTER FOUR

Born in the Malaise

For most of my adult life, I've been frustrated by the fact that ministry has played second fiddle to the administrative and managerial work of being a pastor. Indeed, pastors in the United States are more inclined to see their job as one of organizational leadership, teaching, and perhaps counseling than they are to see it as one of prayer. And lay parishioners, including members of sessions, church councils, elders, diaconate committees, and boards of trustees, are inclined to agree. Most ministerial job descriptions, perhaps especially youth ministry positions, are characterized by strategy, method, vision, goals, and responsibilities (lists and lists of them). Few, if any, ministerial job descriptions explicate prayer as a primary vocation of the minister. Pastors are expected to grow the church, reach the younger generations, supervise the staff and volunteers, teach Bible studies, and preach good sermons. Does your church's pastor or youth minister job description even mention the word *prayer*? And yet, according to Andrew Root, in our secular age, the primary task of the pastor is prayer—"to teach people to pray, and . . . to form her own life around the practice of prayer."[1]

Why has prayer been relegated to a secondary task, something you may or may not mention as one among other pastoral responsibilities? Is it because prayer is difficult? Or is prayer difficult because it has been so relegated? In any case, it is demonstrable that prayer is difficult.

I have been a youth worker for my entire career. And I do say *have been*, not *was*. I still consider myself a youth worker, even now, as the senior pastor of a church. Now, I am *at least* a youth worker, even though I've got other responsibilities too. Young people are part of my community, and therefore they are people to whom I, as a minister, am called to minister. I have outlined elsewhere my view of youth ministry, but for this space, suffice it to say I believe that young people are fully human, full members of the body of Christ, and I believe that ministry is about joining in God's ministry.[2] As such, it cannot be viewed as a top-down minister-to-subject practice. Rather, ministry involves mutuality. It involves the expectation that the same Holy Spirit that is alive in the minister is alive in the one to whom they minister, and therefore ministry is about encountering God in people's concrete and lived experience. The same Holy Spirit that is alive in me, in my church, in my community, in the world is alive in young people—not a junior Holy Spirit, but *the* Holy Spirit, in all her glory! If I am not a youth worker, then I'm missing out on the work of the Holy Spirit.

So, as youth workers (that includes pastors, parents, teachers, adults, and all people who live in the world among young people), it's fundamentally important that we consider how the cross-pressure of the secular age, along with the instrumental rationality of late modernity, has profoundly affected the lives of those born into it, even more so than it has affected us. Prayer is difficult for everyone living in a secular age, but younger generations have distinctive challenges.

WHY PRAYER IS DIFFICULT FOR YOUNG PEOPLE

Millennials, also known as Generation Y, are people born roughly between 1981 and 1996. This generation came of age during the rise of the internet, social media, and mobile technology. Known for being tech savvy, values driven, and collaborative, Millennials are often characterized by their desire for meaningful work, flexibility, and a balanced work-life approach. They experienced key events like the 2008 financial crisis and the rise of digital culture, which influenced their attitudes toward work, education, and social issues.

Generation Z, or Gen Z, refers to people born roughly between 1997 and 2012, coming after Millennials and before Generation Alpha (2013 onward). Having grown up in the age of smartphones, social media, and rapid technological advances, Gen Z has been dubbed the first "digital native" generation and is highly comfortable with technology. They expect constant connectivity and use digital platforms to express themselves, connect, and stay informed. Many Gen Z individuals are passionate about social and environmental causes. They tend to be vocal about issues like climate change, racial and gender equality, and mental health, and they often demand accountability from companies and leaders. Compared to previous generations, Gen Z shows a strong interest in entrepreneurship and freelance work. Many seek flexible work that allows for creativity and independence, likely influenced by exposure to social media platforms where individuals create personal brands or businesses.[3]

It doesn't take special research skills to see that the Millennial and Z generations have some unique mental health challenges or at least that the members of those generations are uniquely aware of their anxiety and depression.[4] While they face unique challenges like social media pressure and the effects of COVID-19 on education and social life, they also tend to be proactive in seeking support and prioritizing self-care. One needs to only spend a few minutes on Instagram or TikTok to see it. Reflecting on her own research, psychologist Lauren Cook writes, "When I started posting on my TikTok to shed light on common disorders such as anxiety, panic attacks, and anxious attachment, I had no idea there would be more than two hundred thousand followers trying to better understand why they were struggling and what they could do about it."[5]

American Millennials have experienced some profound world events that certainly contribute to anxiety and depression—the Columbine High School shooting, 9/11, climate change, economic recession, the Donald Trump presidency, racially motivated police brutality, the January 6 insurrection, mass shootings, homophobia, a global pandemic, the Israeli/Palestinian hostilities, the other Donald Trump presidency—the list goes on. There are lots of reasons Millennials struggle in the malaise of modernity. But Gen Z was *born* of this. Gen Z has not known a world ungoverned by the realities of gun violence, racism, global unrest, rampant conspiracy theories, technological acceleration, and the decay of public trust in institutions.

At the same time, even in this chaotic and uncertain world, these generations are on the cutting edge of social acceleration. The world is ever before them. They have unprecedented access to the world (even if they are no better informed because of it). Theorist Byung-Chul Han has observed that this access has not, in fact, created community but harmed it, creating a poverty of experience. Abundance of information has not led to communication; rather, storytelling has been commodified into "storyselling," and "community without communication gives way to communication without community."[6] As Han puts it, "When all experience is *present and distanceless*, that is, when it is *available*, remembrance is impossible."[7] When every experience is immediately accessible, such as through digital media or on-demand content, it loses a sense of distance or separation from the present moment. In the past, memories were inherently separated from the present because we could only recall them mentally, creating a gap that allowed for nostalgia, reflection, or personal interpretation. This "distanceless" availability means that instead of recalling and interpreting experiences from a mental or emotional distance, we constantly have instant access to them, often in a superficial form (e.g., photos, social media posts). This diminishes the need—and perhaps even the ability—to remember them in a deep, contemplative way. Experiences become like items in an archive rather than cherished memories shaped by time and perspective. "Modernity," writes Han, "is characterized by the demolition of farness, the place of which is taken by gaplessness."[8] They can see images in real time of historic events that would have, in generations past, taken days or weeks to get to them.

But this gaplessness, this accessibility, does not create nearness or resonance with others or with God. Instead, the availability of the world and information actually prevents the nearness of relationship and personhood, according to Han. Information negates personhood because personhood requires mystery, and resonance requires a kind of unknowability and uncontrollability. This is especially true regarding God, who is beyond human knowledge and definitively uncontrollable. Unlike mere physical or emotional proximity, real nearness acknowledges distance, allowing for anticipation, longing, and appreciation. Without these subtle spaces, nearness loses its depth and becomes flat or superficial. As Han writes, "Gaplessness destroys nearness as well as distance. Nearness is not the same as gaplessness, because distance is inscribed in nearness."[9] *Gaplessness* refers to an uninterrupted, constant connection, which paradoxically eliminates both genuine closeness and meaningful distance. Both Gen Z and Millennials are shaped by a society that has lost nearness by removing farness and making the world accessible. They've grown up in a world without mystery or meaning and therefore without prayer.

Of Millennials and Gen Z, market researcher Sarah Weise notes, "These two generations, only a few years apart, both embrace technology, and have become accustomed to on-demand services from transportation to food delivery to streaming television. They share an addiction to social media and the sleep deprivation that goes with it. . . . They both have instant visibility into the lives of others, acquaintances and influencers alike, and they expect active engagement and co-creation with brands. They both want to do good in the world."[10]

Modernity is a result of the fear of having *less* control of the world.[11] Thus, the project of modernity is to bring more and more of the world under our control. "*Our life will be better if we manage to bring more world within our reach*: this is the mantra of modern life, unspoken but relentlessly reiterated and reified in our actions and behavior."[12]

In the chaos of the aforementioned life experiences—recession, gun violence, racism, threats on democracy, the decline of US systems and institutions—the modern project seems hopeless. Yet the demand for immanence is alive and well. These generations are simultaneously witnessing the decline of and the doubling down on the project of modernity. They are cross-pressured by the knowledge that the world is fundamentally out of control and the compulsion to control it. All of this is a product of secularization, and it is more than just an aspect of the Gen Z and Millennial experience; it is the fabric of their experience.

WHAT IS PRAYER?

Many theologians have offered good and useful definitions of prayer. James Martin, for example, documents and explores several definitions in his helpful book *Learning to Pray*.[13] What comes through in his exploration is that we can benefit from multiple definitions that have been handed down to us. According to Martin, "No one definition can fully sum up prayer, but each one captures something important about it. It is a raising up of our minds and hearts; a surge of the heart; sharing between friends; a long, loving look at the real; and a conscious conversation."[14] Thus, it is not my intention to offer a singular and totalizing definition of prayer, especially not in such a limited space. But every appropriate theological definition of prayer requires reliance on, a centering of, and faith in a divine agent.

Of course, there are human elements. Human beings must at some level, even if only secondarily, be receptive to prayer. But definitions of prayer that focus too squarely on what humans are doing when they pray need to be balanced by definitions that adequately consider the centrality and primacy of what God is doing, with or without human participation. To some, the way I have already begun to frame this may be perplexing. I have already hinted that I consider human agency to be of secondary consideration in prayer, but it is our mode of operation to think of prayer as a human action, a discipline, something humans do. God may be out there, but we're the ones *doing* the praying. If I have already implicitly flipped the script, that is explicitly what I intend to do in what follows. When we think of prayer, we must first think of it as something God does, something God initiates. Human beings do not initiate prayer, even if they do participate in it.

Reflecting on St. John Damascene's definition of prayer as "the raising of one's mind and heart to God or the requesting of good things from God," Martin writes, "Overall, St. John's definition is helpful, but it's also incomplete because it is somewhat one-sided. While you're doing the 'raising' and the 'asking,' what is God doing? It seems to omit God's response."[15] Prayer is a communion of God with creation, graciously initiated and sustained by God. According to Jürgen Moltmann, we must put neither the "soul" nor the "world" at the center of prayer: "The center has to be *God* . . . We hope for the *kingdom of God*. That is first and foremost a hope for God, the hope that God will arrive at his rights in his creation, at his peace in his sabbath, and at his eternal joy in his image, human beings."[16] It is God's arrival, God's self-disclosure, God's action that completes any definition of prayer.

God's primacy, as the initiating and sustaining actor, only *compels* human participation in prayer. It does not hinder it. When we've fully understood the costliness of God's action, we cannot help but pray. When we have understood the cost of God's coming to us—the cost, indeed, of the cross—not as an abstract principle, the "data for our calculations," but as the "answer to a sum" of Christ's achievement in reconciling us to God, then we discover that prayer requires our participation.[17] When we grasp the depth of God's self-giving love, poured out for us in Christ, prayer becomes not a duty but a natural response. It is our humble *yes* to the one who has already reached out in grace, drawing us into communion. In this light, prayer is not an obligation imposed on us but a gift—an invitation to step into the mystery of God's ongoing work in us and through us. Thus, the short answer to the question "What is prayer?" can be summed up in the word *gift* but must be nuanced, in all seriousness, by the truth of the costliness of this gift, a cost to the giver that compels a response from the recipient.

EVEN YOUTHS GROW TIRED

The secular age makes the necessary epistemic centralization of God all but impossible. How do we center God's action when we can hardly even conceive of a God who acts? Andrew Root and Blair Bertrand note that "the secular age blinds us to God's action, but, even further, it makes the very possibility of God's action impossible to imagine."[18] This is partly why prayer is so difficult for us. We think it is a discipline we must master instead of a shared encounter of the divine and human. Because it is so difficult for us to imagine a God who acts, "all we are left with is our action."[19] Our lives are no longer defined by faithfulness to an other. We are now what Han calls "an achievement society" that suffers from "excessive positivity," governed not by a *should* but a *can*, in which everything is possible and *must* be possible only for the human being (since there is no one else with agency in this frame of thinking).[20] If it needs to be done and has not yet been done, then *we* can and must do it. In short, we are exhausted. Young people feel this exhaustion acutely, though their indigeneity to its ecosystem may disguise its effects.

Prayer becomes just one more task, one more thing people must do, another skill we must achieve, a discipline we must master. The conditions of human action are bleak in a world where instrumental reason and capitalist optimization have become the governing rationalities of human agency. In this context, prayer can only be seen from the human side of the equation. Prayer becomes a human action, measured according to its contribution to the meeting of a desired outcome. Divine action is missing. Prayer is, then, motivated not by joy or faithfulness but by effectiveness. It is works, not grace. Because we can and must do it, what matters is what our doing produces. Thus, prayer and the world itself, as a world defined by immanence and human agency, become what Hartmut Rosa calls "a point of aggression."[21] When young people pray, their secular context presents it as a skill to be aggressively acquired and mastered.

Why is this the case? Perhaps it is connected to the problem from which this chapter began. Prayer is considered secondary even to the pastoral vocation, and people—including young people—are watching. If prayer were seen as more than just one task among others, perhaps our ears might hear a different question. Perhaps the question "How is your prayer life?" could be interpreted not as a test of faithfulness, like a dentist asking how much you floss, but as an invitation to narrate your experience of God. If prayer were seen as a divine action, and not merely a human one, we might see the question of prayer as a question of God's faithfulness and an opportunity to see where and how God has been active in the world and in one's life.

DEVELOPMENTALISM AND DYNAMIC STABILIZATION

This leads to another element of secularization that may be considered even more fundamental to young people's experience: what Rosa calls "dynamic stabilization." According to Rosa, "A modern society . . . is one that can stabilize itself only dynamically, in other words one that requires constant economic growth, technological acceleration, and cultural innovation in order to maintain its institutional status quo."[22] This dynamic stabilization is defined by a need for progress. Indeed, everything in this epistemic frame is valued on a scale of decline and improvement. If something is not improving, it is declining. This makes sense because, as Han puts it, "when reference to the Other goes missing, no stable self-image can form."[23] In my own work, I have looked in detail at this dynamic stabilization. There, I have called it—in broad terms—*developmentalism*, defined as "a hermeneutical framework that situates human life—and history itself—on a progressive trajectory and a qualitative scale of improvement."[24]

Developmentalism and dynamic stabilization cannot sit still.

PRAYER AS A GIFT OF THE MOMENT

Prayer is not about optimization for future development, and it is not a discipline to be mastered. It is a gift of the moment. It is a gift of

Hartmut Rosa's resonance. Andrew Root reminds us that "resonance is when you experience your own life teeming with meaning. But it's meaning that seems to be coming to you." Artist and writer Jenny Odell reflects on her own experience: "The happiest, most fulfilled moments of my life have been when I was completely aware of being alive, with all the hope, pain, and sorrow that that entails for any mortal being. In those moments, the idea of success as a teleological goal would have made no sense; the moments were ends in themselves, not steps on a ladder."[25]

Resonance—and prayer as resonance—is an end in itself. According to Rosa, "In contrast to what happens in the practices of alchemy or magic, in prayer there is no attempt to manipulate the other side or engineer a particular result."[26] Resonance is about reachability, not controllability. And while God cannot be controlled because God is love (1 John 4:8 and 16), God can be reached. Or, to put it more precisely, God can reach us. It is the being reached, the being with, that defines the true end of the Christian practice of prayer. It is God with us in the person of Jesus Christ that constitutes prayer. The trajectory, then, is not from us to God; it is from God to us. It is not something we acquire through our own ambition; it is something disclosed to us. Prayer as resonance is action in the *being* mode of existence. Erich Fromm explains, "Because the society we live in is devoted to acquiring property and making a profit, we rarely see any evidence of the being mode of existence and most people see the having mode as the most natural mode of existence, even the only acceptable way of life."[27]

When prayer is a point of aggression, a human action for optimization toward dynamic stabilization and development, prayer becomes a possession. In modernity, we *have* a prayer life; we are not *in prayer*. This may be key to understanding the absurdity of the apostle Paul's instruction to "pray without ceasing" (1 Thess 5:17). If prayer is something we "have"—a skill we must acquire or a habit we must form—then to pray without ceasing is a burdensome proposition. But if prayer is something of the *being* mode of existence, then even when our action cannot be described as "praying," we may find ourselves *in* prayer—in that experience of communion with God, abiding in us, in resonance.

Prayer as a gift of the moment, as being and resonance, is more akin to bird-watching or falling asleep than it is to learning to speak German.[28] As Rosa points out, "The harder we try [to fall asleep], the less we succeed."[29] Resonance is not under control, even if there are ways in which we can position ourselves to receive it. With falling asleep, maybe putting on some lullabies or making sure one's CPAP mask is properly connected (for those of us who need to use such a device, of course) will put one in a better position to fall asleep, but even with these conditions, sleep is no guarantee.

Perhaps an even more appropriate metaphor, particularly regarding prayer as resonance, is that of bird-watching.[30] In bird-watching, the watcher is in the position of one who waits. We can put ourselves in the right position to notice birds. We may even be able to find ways of attracting them, but we cannot compel the birds to reveal themselves to us. An attempt to control the birds would likely be counterproductive. As Rosa says, "Attempting to take hold of the dynamic of resonance generally means *paralyzing* it."[31] In the end, birds are seen not by discovery but through disclosure. Similarly, God is knowable but not controllable.

The Hebrew Scriptures give testament to God's uncontrollability. Solomon asked, "Who is able to build a temple for [God], since the heavens, even the highest heavens, cannot contain [God]?" (2 Chron 2:6). The prophet Isaiah gives an answer from God's own voice: "'Heaven is my throne, and the earth is my footstool. Where is the house you will build for me? Where will my resting place be? Has not my hand made all these things, and so they came into being?' declares the Lord" (Isa 66:1–2). And the author of Lamentations asks, "Who can speak and have it happen if the Lord has not decreed it?" (Lam 3:37). In the New Testament, the Gospel of John, its famous third chapter, gives voice to the uncontrollability of God: "The wind blows wherever it pleases. You hear its sound, but you cannot tell where it comes from or where it is going. So it is with everyone born of the Spirit" (John 3:8). Prayer, throughout the Scriptures, is not an act of control. "When you pray," Jesus says, according to Matthew, "do not keep talking on and on the way ungodly people do. They think they will be heard because they talk a lot. Do not be like them. Your Father knows what you need even before you ask" (Matt 6:7–8). Prayer is about waiting on God and abiding in Christ as Christ abides in us (John 15:4–11): "Humans are supposed to *listen* to God or *hear* God's word, and God in turn can be reached through prayer—although this precisely does not mean that he [*sic*] can in any way be controlled."[32]

In light of secularization, then, the plethora of reasons that prayer would be found difficult by Gen Z and Millennials is evident. If our epistemology is characterized by the contestability of transcendence and a prioritization of the immanent, if our horizon has disappeared and yet we cannot help but strive, if the lack of a divine agent has forced us to grasp for control of an uncontrollable world, then how is prayer even a possibility for us? But it is especially in light of these realities, in this context and to young people's experience, that prayer is fundamental.

In what may be the greatest work on prayer written in the past twenty years, *God, Sexuality, and the Self*, Sarah Coakley writes, "What is blanked out in the regular, patient attempt to attend to God in prayer is *any* sense of human grasp; and what comes to replace such an ambition, over time, is the elusive, but nonetheless ineluctable, sense of *being grasped*, of the Spirit's simultaneous erasure of human idolatry and subtle reconstitution of human selfhood in God."[33]

In prayer lies the promise of liberation. Young people need prayer, and they (we) need to be taught how to pray. This, then, makes the pastoral vocation of prayer that much more urgent in the lives of young people. In our society of achievement and developmentalism, this is easier said than done. The *action* of "being grasped" by the "reconstitution of human selfhood" is not an action of the type we are accustomed to doing. It is not characterized by strategy, method, goals, and responsibility. It is not a point of aggression. For us to recentralize prayer as a pastoral vocation to meet the needs of young people who are being crushed under the weight of excessive positivity, we will need to learn to wait, to abide, and to allow God to act.

Abiding in the Moment

In a world that celebrates speed, productivity, and constant movement, it's easy to feel swept up in the demand to always be *doing*—striving, achieving, and progressing. But what if the stability we seek isn't found in dynamic movement or constant becoming but in being still? In simply *being*—grounded in the presence of God, who comes to us where we are, as we are. Prayer invites us into this space of stability, not through effort or mastery but through resting in God's grace and presence.

This truth echoes the psalmist's words in Psalm 46:10: "Be still, and know that I am God." It's a call not to accomplish or prove but to pause and rest, trusting in God's sustaining presence. The God who creates and redeems also comes to stabilize us—not through our striving but through divine love that meets us in the present.

In prayer, we learn to let go of the need to control or perfect ourselves. We discover that God's work is not about pushing us toward a distant or abstract ideal but about transforming the imperfections of our lives into something good. We are invited to embrace the now, to see God at work in our surroundings and within us.

The following prayer practice can be done individually or with a group. It is a way to cultivate attentiveness to the present moment and to the sacredness of what is around us.

1. *Prepare*
   Begin in a quiet place where you can sit or stand comfortably. If you're with a group, gather in a circle. Take a few deep breaths, allowing yourself to settle. Close your eyes if you feel comfortable or soften your gaze.
2. *Centering*
   Start with a simple phrase or prayer to center yourself: "God, open my eyes to see your presence around me. Help me to be where my feet are, fully here, in this moment."

3. *Notice the Present Moment*

   Take a minute to observe your surroundings. If you're outside or near a window, notice the sounds of birds, the rustle of leaves, or the warmth of the sun. If you're indoors, notice the texture of the chair, the faint hum of the room, the smell of coffee or whatever aroma fills your space. Or notice the faces of those gathered with you. As you notice each element, silently thank God for it: "Thank you for this sound, for this sight, for this moment."
4. *Breath Prayer*

   Extend your hands outward, palms up, as a symbol of openness. As you do, say, "God, I open myself to your presence." Slowly bring your hands to your heart, palms resting over it, and say, "Help me to receive your peace and love."

   If you're with a group, you may choose to extend your hands toward others as a gesture of connection and blessing: "Help me to receive your peace and love."
5. *Conclude with Gratitude*

   End the practice by expressing gratitude. If in a group, invite each person to name something they noticed or appreciated. If alone, silently or aloud, or perhaps in a journal or on a sheet of paper, name what you are thankful for.

   Close with a prayer: "God, thank you for this time to slow down, to notice, and to be present. Help me carry this awareness into the rest of my day."

By slowing down in prayer, we open ourselves to God's stabilizing presence, not as something we achieve but as a gift we receive. It's a way of simply *being*—grounded in the grace of the one who comes to us.

Amen.

CHAPTER FIVE

Playing Better Games

It started innocently enough, as most church disputes do. The session at a small Presbyterian church in Indiana was meeting to discuss a series of minor renovations, one of which included replacing the old, threadbare carpet in the sanctuary. A small subcommittee had been formed to handle the details: Sarah, the artistic head of the worship committee, who herself had worked in interior design; Bill, a longtime elder with a penchant for pragmatism; and Jane, a new member of the church with a keen eye for design but no formal education or experience in it.

Sarah had suggested they go with a deep burgundy, a color she felt would add warmth and reverence to the sanctuary. It would also look nice during Pentecost, when the paraments would be red (her favorite time in the church year). Bill, ever the traditionalist, argued for a classic navy blue, a color that he said exuded dignity and timelessness. Jane, who wanted to make her mark, proposed a vibrant green to symbolize growth and renewal. Each argument was well-intentioned, and initially, discussions were polite and respectful. However, as weeks passed, it proved difficult for the group to decide, and the debate grew heated. Sarah and Bill could not see eye to eye, each convinced that their choice was the only appropriate one. Jane, feeling marginalized, rallied support among newer and younger members who were less involved in the leadership but shared her vision for what they considered to be a more vibrant and contemporary look. What began as a disagreement among three people quickly spread. Session meetings became battlegrounds, with members taking sides. Discussions that should have been focused on the church's mission and ministry were dominated by the carpet issue. The once cohesive group of leaders found themselves divided, and their unity was being tested in ways they had not anticipated. The congregation, too, began to feel the strain. People gossiped about the arguments, and Sunday coffee hours became forums for debate. Members who had once been friends found themselves avoiding each other. The youth group—who had little collective interest in the color of the carpet in the sanctuary—tried to make light of it, joking in the background about Team Burgundy, Team Navy, and Team Green, but even they felt the tension in the air.

Rev. James, the church's pastor, watched with growing concern. He had tried to recuse himself from the debate and hoped that the new carpet would be a simple decision. He even saw it as superficial. Doesn't the church have bigger fish to fry? Hadn't Rev. James's education—in which he was so deeply engaged in questions about the history and future of the world, the divinity of Christ, the authority of the Scriptures, and the depth of reality itself—prepared him for more important issues than the color of the carpet? But the carpet issue seemed to be far more "relevant" and divisive than any theological issue he'd ever dealt with. It seemed like it was tearing the church apart.

During one particularly contentious session meeting, he decided enough was enough. "Friends," Rev. James began, standing to address the group, "we have lost sight of what is truly important. We are here to serve God and be a blessing to our community, not to argue over the color of the carpet. This decision should not divide us." There was a pregnant pause, a few blank stares, and an air of confusion. No one seemed to know how to respond. Of course, Rev. James was right, and everyone knew it. But isn't it *easier* to deal with the carpet than to try to talk about something as nebulous as "serving God"?

After a few moments of quiet, someone on the opposite side of the room took a breath and said, "Well, I guess I could be convinced to switch to burgundy." And the argument continued.

STUPID GAMES, STUPID PRIZES

If you've been in church leadership for any amount of time, or even been a member of a church, you probably have a story like this one (or several of them). Churches can be places of deep and profound meaning, where people are empowered to do incredible things for themselves and their communities, where they encounter the love of God and experience hope and joy. But inevitably, it seems, they are plagued by petty arguments and silly superficial concerns. Even the concerns we take to be serious ones are too often void of theology and drenched in secular and institutional anxiety over influence, numbers, and rules. I've always found it disheartening that, even among Christian educators and theologians, superficial concern over the survival of the institutional church and shallow obsession over tactics and strategies have dominated over deeper discussions about the gospel and all its theological import, discussions that cut to the heart of reality itself.

When we should be talking about the crisis of faith, we tend to talk more about the crisis of effectiveness.[1] When we find ourselves consumed by petty concerns, we're going to end up having petty conflicts, like the carpet issue. When we're obsessed with a concern over having less power—when we feel threatened by secularization—we will end up obsessed by the desire for more. This, of course, has been the reaction of the religious right, characterized by a fear of "losing the culture." These petty superficialities and institutional anxieties have pulled the rug from under the church's ministry and mission. Play stupid games, win stupid prizes.

DEVOTE YOURSELVES TO PRAYER

At the end of Paul's letter to the Colossians, he leaves his audience with two perplexing closing instructions—perplexing because they seem somewhat out of place, at least to the modern reader. The letter is addressed to a group of Christians, a church in the city of Colossae, in a region called Phrygia—not too far from the larger, more famous city of Laodicea. In Phrygia, there existed a plurality of theological and religious traditions and practices—competing philosophies that were surely part of Paul's motivation for writing the letter. According to Craig S. Keener, "Religion was practiced with intensity and sometimes frenzy."[2] The Colossians were likely confused and probably feeling a little threatened. Their new religion, Christianity—led by prisoners, slaves, and women—was under pressure to assert itself. If we were to try to place ourselves in that situation, we could imagine feeling the need to "win the culture" and try to "fight" for the position of Christian theology over and against these competing religions and pagan ideals. The voice of the gospel of Jesus Christ was being drowned out by the sea of voices saying, "Do this, do that; believe this, eat that, wear this, worship that."

So Paul speaks out in his letter, reminding them of the mystery of Christ. He reminds them that Jesus, the one who was tortured and crucified, was, in fact, supreme over all creation and the "image of the invisible God." He reminds them that they need nothing other than Jesus, that the virtues that might win them social or religious power are, in fact, superseded by the virtues of compassion, kindness, humility, gentleness, and patience (virtues that are hardly helpful in a culture war). And then, in the final chapter, when one might hope to gain some helpful tips about gaining control over the situation and taming the frenzied religious culture, converting the heathens, Paul says, "Devote yourselves to prayer" (Col 4:2 NIV).

Really? Prayer! That's Paul's closing argument?

In our modern society, we'd take that to be a disingenuous suggestion: "Yes, I see that you're losing ground, that your institution is under threat, that the gospel is being syncretized by all of these different competing religions and philosophies. You should pray about it." We'd probably scoff.

Of course, we'd have room to scoff since far too often people have used "thoughts and prayers" as an antithesis to action and an excuse to avoid confronting systemic injustices. But nevertheless, that is Paul's instruction—"devote yourselves to prayer, being watchful and thankful" (Col 4:2 NIV). He doesn't ask them to look away from their problem, but he doesn't ask them to rage against the machine, either. He asks them to pray, to devote themselves to prayer.

Then, a little later, he does something even stranger. He says, "I, Paul, write this greeting in my own hand" (Col 4:18 NIV), suggesting that perhaps he had been allowing a scribe to take down the letter up to this point. One might imagine Paul snatching the pen from the hand of the scribe for this one last important line: "Remember my chains" (Col 4:18 NIV).

With his last line, in his own handwriting, he reminds them that they're receiving this letter not from some dignitary, not from someone who has won a culture war or achieved some worldly status or authority, but from a prisoner. The gospel, he reminds them, is not a religion of power. It is a religion centered on the worship and supremacy of a crucified God. It is the religion of Jesus, the Nazarene who was tortured and executed, who is served not by kings and kingmakers but by prisoners in chains. And Paul isn't the kind of prisoner who fights or has some scheme to regain his status or escape his fate. You can read about it in Acts 16: When Paul goes to prison, he sings hymns. Losing—the experience of failure, weakness, or sacrifice—is not contrary to Christianity. We are free, not to win power but to pray, to have grace-filled conversation, to wear love like a garment: "Grace be with you" (Col 4:18 NIV).

BETTER GAMES, BETTER PRIZES?

The truth is that we as human beings—and, thus, we in the church—are wired for conflict. We're created for deep and meaningful "games." We are so wired for the "right," for good and for love—being in the image of God—that it is our true nature to rail against the things that are not right, good, or loving. In Jürgen Moltmann's words, "Those who hope in Christ can no longer put up with reality as it is, but begin to suffer under it, to contradict it. Peace with God means conflict with the world, for the goad of the promised future stabs inexorably into the flesh of every unfulfilled present."[3] What happens, however, is our alignment gets thrown off. Our railing becomes misdirected, and our capacity for conflict becomes destructive, petty, and superficial.

In our secular age, we have lost our confidence in dealing with the real and better games of transcendence. We don't feel like we can deal with the mysterious challenges at the heart of reality—the crises of faith. Douglas John Hall notes, "We are not confident that our ecclesiastical loyalty—or even our faith—could stand exposure to the data that is present in contemporary experience."[4] Hall goes on to say, "Neither as a religion nor as a people can we cope with the questions that history has thrown up to us."[5] So, rather than try to cope with those questions or embrace the mystery of reality, we have pursued unreality instead. While the church *should* be concerned about the more transcendent crises of our world—or perhaps more directly with the crisis of secularization itself—we have misdirected our railings toward the imminent and superficial "crises" around us, like our institutional effectiveness and sustainability, the color of the carpet, or the preparation of the coffee for fellowship hour: "We want a world in which problems are solvable—chiefly by technological means. We want to believe *ourselves* to be the bearers of the solution, of salvation!"[6] So if there's a problem we can't control, we are tempted to set it aside and deal only with problems we can get our hands around. Theologically, however, if it's a problem that human beings can handle on their own, it probably isn't that important, and the "prize" probably isn't worth winning.

When we limit ourselves to immanence and to the things we can control, we easily begin to value things only according to their usefulness in giving us control. This is how the immanent frame has led to instrumental rationality. Thus, prayer itself is either redefined as an instrument (we pray only for solutions to problems and judge prayer by its immanent outcomes) or else it loses its value altogether. Prayer as a ceding of control, prayer as amen—offering control to God and waiting on God's action—seems like a waste of time (and, according to instrumental rationality, it probably is).

PRAYER AS CHRISTOPRAXIS

The movement of prayer is the movement out of instrumental rationality and into what Jürgen Moltmann, Ray Anderson, and Andrew Root have called *Christopraxis*. To understand Christopraxis, we need a little background on Aristotle.

Aristotle's philosophy, though rooted in ancient Greece and not in Christian thought, has profoundly shaped the way we understand human action, ethics, and society, influencing the development of modernity. His ideas on virtue, rationality, and the purpose of human life—particularly through his concept of *telos* (purpose or end)—laid the groundwork for much of Western thought, including Christian theology. Aristotle's emphasis on practical reason and ethical living informed later thinkers, from Augustine to Aquinas, and provided a framework for understanding human agency, decision-making, and the moral life. In the context of modernity, Aristotle's insights help us grasp the evolution of ideas about autonomy, individualism, and the pursuit of happiness, all central themes in modern philosophical and political discourse. His exploration of human nature and action offers key tools for engaging with modern questions about the self, ethics, and the common good.

In Aristotle's philosophy, the concepts of *poiesis* and *praxis* refer to different types of activities and their purposes. *Poiesis*, derived from the Greek word for *making* or *production*, involves activities that result in an end product separate from the activity itself. The focus of *poiesis* is on the creation or production of something tangible or intangible, such as a piece of art, a tool, or a poem. Examples of *poiesis* include a carpenter building a chair or a musician composing a song. In contrast, *praxis*, derived from the Greek word for *action* or *practice*, involves activities that are ends in themselves, where the purpose is the activity itself rather than an external product. The goal of *praxis* is the performance of the activity, often with a focus on ethical or moral action and the development of character and virtue. Examples of *praxis* include engaging in ethical deliberation, participating in political life, or acting justly. The key difference between the two lies in their outcomes: *Poiesis* results in an external product, while *praxis* is an activity where the doing itself is the purpose. Aristotle emphasized the importance of *praxis* in achieving *eudaimonia*, or human flourishing, as it involves living a virtuous and ethical life through actions that are inherently valuable.

Jürgen Moltmann introduced the term *Christopraxis* in his 1978 work *The Church in the Power of the Spirit*. In this book, Moltmann explores the idea of a Christian praxis (practice) that is centered on the life and mission of Christ, emphasizing the active, transformative role of the church in the world. The concept of Christopraxis reflects Moltmann's emphasis on a theology that is not merely theoretical but is lived out in the practical, ethical actions of Christians as they participate in God's work in the world. The term really gained prominence and more definition through the work of Ray S. Anderson, a theologian known for his contributions to practical theology.[7] Anderson emphasizes the active, transformative presence of Christ in the practices of the church and the lives of believers, coining the term to describe a theological approach that integrates theological reflection with practical action.

Anderson's articulation of Christopraxis was later expanded and explored by other theologians, including Root.[8] As defined by Root, Christopraxis refers to a theological approach that emphasizes the active presence and work of Christ in the world through the practices of the church and the lives of believers. This concept integrates the theological (Christ's action) and the practical (human action), focusing on how Christ's transformative action is made manifest in concrete, lived experience. Central to Christopraxis is the idea of incarnational presence, underscoring the ongoing incarnation of Christ in the world, where the church acts as the body of Christ, engaging in actions that participate in Christ's ministry. People are seen as participants in Christ's redemptive work, engaging in practices that embody the love, justice, and reconciliation of Christ. Christopraxis involves a transformative engagement with the world, where theological reflection and practical action are intertwined, aiming to bring about personal and social transformation in alignment with the values of the kingdom of God. It is not just about theoretical knowledge but also about lived faith that actively participates in God's redemptive work in the world.

Root's distinctive contribution to the conversation about Christopraxis lies in his exploration of how the cross of Christ can serve as a central framework for understanding and practicing ministry. His work builds on the foundation laid by earlier theologians like Anderson but takes it in a nuanced direction by emphasizing the implications of Christ's suffering and the movement from death to life for practical theology. Root's key contribution is his development of a practical theology of the cross, which redefines Christian ministry through the lens of the event of the revelation of God through Christ's suffering and death. He argues that the cross is not just a historical event but also a paradigm for understanding how Christians should engage in ministry and live out their faith in the world. Root posits that ministry is Christopraxis, the work of participating in Christ's ministry as an end in itself.

In *Christopraxis*, Root explores these themes through various case studies and theological reflections. For example, he discusses how ministry can be reframed as a form of participation in the suffering of the world, drawing from both historical and contemporary examples to illustrate how the cross serves as a guide for practical theological work. Throughout, Root's distinctive contribution to the conversation about Christopraxis is his focus on the cross of Christ as a central motif for understanding and practicing Christian ministry. Root's approach emphasizes suffering, sacrifice, and solidarity as core components of a transformative and just ministry practice. Ministry must be empathetic, engaging with the realities of others' experiences of suffering. He challenges ministry practices that focus on *poiesis*—outcomes of growth and success—advocating instead for a model that embodies the cross's message of God's gracious work in the impossibility of human action. In other words, Christopraxis, like prayer, cedes control and embraces our existential lack of control. Christopraxis is, essentially, prayer itself. It is the communal and communicative immersion in and dependence on the person of Jesus Christ. Christopraxis as ministry is human action that is drenched in prayer—enveloped, determined, and substantiated on the grace of the God who raised Christ from the dead. It is shaped like the hypostatic union, a concept we'll further explore later, wherein human action is taken into the very life and being of God and gifted back to the human being *as* the life and being of God. We call this work *ministry*. And this ministry is prayer.

One of the dreams I have for my own church in Ramona, California, is to be a praying church, to "devote ourselves to prayer." What I mean by being a praying church isn't that we would constantly stop to say prayers together or even that individuals would be constantly praying on their own. I do hope for that, too, but what I really hope for, what I really mean when I say I want us to become a praying church, is that I want us to understand our activity not in terms of instrumental outcomes or poiesitic practices aimed at achieving specific goals but through the lens of divine praxis—the ongoing work of Christ through the power of the Holy Spirit. In other words, I want us to frame our actions as participation in God's continuous action, seeing ministry not as a means to an end but as an end in itself. To be a praying church is to embrace Christopraxis, relinquishing control and surrendering the outcomes of our work to the God who raised Jesus from death to life. It means taking ourselves less seriously as the actors or controllers of the church and more seriously as humble participants dependent on the person and work of Christ in the world.

COFFEE WARS

In this uncontrollable world, what tends to happen when we don't see ministry as Christopraxis, when we're not a praying church, is that we get bogged down in the things we *can* control but that ultimately don't matter very much. We make mountains out of mole hills, and the church becomes about products and resources rather than the love and compassion that give meaning to any good product or resource.

Instead of "wasting" our time on things that matter but don't have clear and measurable outcomes, we waste our time on things that don't matter but do have clear and measurable outcomes—things like the color of the carpet and the distribution of the coffee during fellowship time.

One of the first disputes I had to navigate when I became the pastor of First Congregational Church of Ramona was one that broke out among the board of diaconate. Our diaconate is the team of people who prepare the sanctuary to be a hospitable place for corporate worship. They change the paraments on the altar, make sure there are enough Kleenex boxes in the pews, get out the accessible-parking signs for the parking spaces in front of the church, assure that people get bulletins and are sufficiently welcomed into the sanctuary, and (most importantly) make sure there's coffee available to the congregation before and after worship gatherings.

I was just getting my feet wet as the pastor of the church, and at one of the first meetings of the board of diaconate, I suggested the coffee might taste better and be more inviting if people had some variety. A Keurig seemed like a good compromise. Not only would it feel welcoming, but it would also save the diaconate some work. True, *real* coffee people (the snobs) would still be disappointed, but at least it'd be better than burnt Folgers. Plus, there'd be some variety. Kids could make hot chocolate, and people could even make hot teas or ciders for themselves if we put it out.

I thought it'd be a welcome idea. I thought it would be noncontroversial to suggest that we put out a couple of Keurig coffee machines instead of the large silver urn of Folgers we'd been putting out for years. I thought it would be an innocuous suggestion.

I was wrong.

The diaconate became divided into factions. Some wanted to keep their urn of burnt Folgers; others had no better suggestions but voiced their disdain for the Keurig. It was too expensive or too wasteful, or the line to get it would be too long because the Keurig wasn't fast enough. Others loved the idea and defended it with their lives. It was anarchy!

The board decided (reluctantly) to give the Keurigs a try and see what kind of feedback we got. For weeks to come, it was the topic of conversations in the parking lot after worship. People who wanted the Keurigs were trying to win people to their side, and people who didn't want them were trying to win people to their side. For months, the same debate ensued at each diaconate meeting and always for way longer than I could have guessed. People were dressed in camouflage and wearing red bandannas, fashioning torches and spears out of the candelabras. It was postapocalyptic!

Okay, that last part may not be true (blame my trauma), but what's definitely true is that I created drama where I did not expect to find it. What had I done? Why was there all this fuss over such a superficial concern? And why was it persisting?

What I had done was give people who lacked other measurable goals something on which they could fixate. I gave people who hadn't really defined their work theologically as *praxis* a welcome distraction of *poiesis*. People who were struggling to grasp the meaning of their work as ministry clung to the coffee war because it gave them something to be passionate about, something they could measure (it's too expensive, it takes too long . . . no, it's less wasteful than throwing away the Folgers every week; it'll take less time to set up, etc., etc.). Because we're wired for a fight, if we don't have an important fight, we'll find an unimportant one to engage in. I gave people a fight, and they jumped in wholeheartedly. The fight would persist, I realized, until we found a more important concern.

It occurred to me that the diaconate didn't actually know why they existed. They thought they did. They thought they existed to set up for worship, change the paraments, put the flowers on the altar, and make sure the coffee was out for fellowship time. But that's just the stuff they do; it's not why they exist. The term *diaconate* refers to the office or position of a deacon within the church. It encompasses the collective body of deacons serving in a particular church. In many traditions, deacons are ordained ministers who often assist in various aspects of church life, including pastoral care, administration, and service to the community. The specific roles and responsibilities of deacons can vary widely among different Christian traditions. The word *diaconate* originates from the Greek word *διάκονος* (*diakonos*), which means *servant* or *minister.* The term was adopted into Latin as *diaconus* and then into Old English as *diacon*, eventually evolving into the modern English word *deacon*. The concept of the diaconate as an office within the church has its roots in early Christian communities, where deacons were appointed to serve and assist in the distribution of alms, care for those in need, and perform other acts of service. Deacons were ministers, participants in Christ's ongoing activity in the world.

The diaconate doesn't exist to change the paraments and put out the coffee. The diaconate exists to serve people, to be ministers. And that's what was missing. The diaconate didn't know that they were ministers, so they got hung up on the coffee. What they needed to understand was that they weren't there to accomplish some goal or perform some tasks. They were there as ministers in the way of Jesus.

So one Sunday, we had the conversation. At the diaconate meeting, just about the point when we'd usually start arguing about the coffee again, I brought it up. "Why are we here?" I asked. "What's our job as diaconate?"

I got some good answers like "Well, we're here to make sure everything is set up for church and cleaned up after church." But then someone said it: "I think our job is hospitality." She said it as though she was surprised that she was saying it, as though she'd realized it no sooner than she'd vocalized it. "Yes," I said, "now that's a theological idea!"

We then dove into a conversation no less passionate, but far less *heated*, than the one about the coffee (no pun intended). We talked about how important it is that people felt the warmth and radical welcome of the Holy Spirit when they walked into the sanctuary for worship, how vital it was that people could encounter one another in fellowship and find God in the relationships of their church family. We talked about what had brought each of us to the church and what kept us coming back. We didn't stop and say a prayer, but we became a praying church because we were beginning to see our work not in the light of our own human tasks but in the light of Christ's work in the world—Christopraxis.

Truth be told, the distribution of the coffee actually *does* matter but not for the reasons some of the members of our board of diaconate thought. We discovered together that the coffee wasn't just a task we had to accomplish for expediency. The reason we have coffee at all is because we value relationships, and we want people to feel welcome. The conversation about the coffee, when it is handled prayerfully as ministry, transforms from an argument about time and money to a discussion about how we can make sure people know that they are loved and cared for.[9] Handled prayerfully and faithfully, work transforms into *ministry* and becomes an end in itself rather than a means to an end. Whether we served burnt Folgers in an urn or put out Keurigs for people, the point isn't the coffee at all. The church does not need better coffee—it needs deeper relationships; it needs the indwelling of the Holy Spirit, an abiding relationship with God. It needs resonance. In short, what the church really needs is ministry—to have our being taken into the being of God, to find ourselves abiding in the faithfulness of Jesus, who goes to the cross out of love for the world, to cultivate a union between the divine and human. The point is *ministry*, and that's a game worth playing.

Abiding in Play

My kids love playgrounds. Our family is grateful that in all the places we've lived together, from coast to coast, there's been a playground close by our home. There's something about walking to the playground and just joining in on the playfulness of children, where the world feels alive with laughter and imagination. What if prayer is about that same kind of joy? Maybe we've made prayer about solemnity and getting stuff done when it's really more about embracing the joy of connection—abiding in the God who lives and moves and plays.

Prayer mustn't be confined to traditional rules or expectations we often feel. Instead, it opens the door to a relationship where you can leave behind the weight of trivial concerns. The unimportant worries that cloud your mind—like the dishes left undone, or the deadlines looming, or the number of butts that were in pews last Sunday—can float away like dandelion seeds in the breeze, giving way to the deeper, more mysterious, yet more meaningful work of God that unfolds in your life and in the life of your church.

1. *Create Your Joyful Space*
   Find a spot that inspires a sense of wonder—a garden, a cozy corner, or even a vibrant park bench. Surround yourself with things that spark joy: colorful flowers, playful artwork, or the sounds of nature. Allow this space to be a sanctuary of lightness where you can freely express your heart.
2. *Embrace Your Body's Rhythm*
   Begin by moving your body—twist, turn, or sway as you feel led. Let the energy of your movements help release any lingering tension or worries. Imagine each movement as a gentle reminder that you are free to connect with God, for God moves with you.
3. *Welcome God's Presence with Joy*
   Take a moment to acknowledge that God is here, right alongside you, delighting in your presence. Imagine God joining you in your dance, inviting you to step into a relationship

marked by joy and imagination. There's no need to reach for God; you're already enveloped in divine love.

4. *Let Go of Perfect Words*
   If words come to you, share them openly but remember there's no pressure to find the "right" ones. Let your prayers flow naturally, whether they express gratitude, joy, or even the lighter side of your worries. If silence feels more appropriate, embrace it. Let the stillness become part of your prayerful dance.
5. *Listen for Whispers of Joy*
   Spend a few moments simply being present. In the stillness, listen for the whispers of God in your heart. You may feel a spark of joy, a sense of peace, or a playful nudge inviting you to see things differently. Allow yourself to be open to God's movement, even if it's not something you can measure or define.
6. *Respond with a Playful Spirit*
   As feelings or thoughts arise, respond with authenticity. Speak to God as a friend, sharing your experiences, worries, or the amusing moments of your day. Know that God delights in your honesty, not for perfection but for your willingness to engage openly.
7. *Rest in the Lightness of God's Love*
   Before concluding your prayer, take a moment to soak in the truth of God's love for you. Feel the warmth of that love wrapping around you, reminding you that it's okay to let go of what doesn't matter. You are cherished just as you are, free to enjoy the relationship you share.
8. *Close with a Spirit of Joy*
   When you're ready to end your time of prayer, do so gently. Bring back your awareness to the world around you, carrying the sense of joy and playfulness with you. As you continue your day, remember that God walks with you, ready to infuse your life with love and light in unexpected ways.

In the grand tapestry of life, the worries that often consume us—whether they're managing church programs, balancing the budget, counting attendance, or even debating the color of the carpet—pale in comparison to the richness of simply being in God's presence. These concerns, while they may feel pressing in the moment, are fleeting and secondary to our call to be faithful stewards of God's love and grace. When we shift our focus away from the minutiae and toward the heart of our relationship with God, we find ourselves empowered to participate in the divine action unfolding around us. It's in this sacred space that we discover our true purpose—not in the numbers or decisions we make but in how we embody God's love in our community and engage with the world, reflecting the joy and hope that God instills within us.

Amen.

CHAPTER SIX

The Paradox of Prayer

It was one of those hot Ramona mornings, the kind that makes the steering wheel burn your hands when you get in the car. It was 10:00 a.m. and already in the nineties, and it was clearly going to reach triple digits before it got any cooler (we tell ourselves it's a "dry heat" so we can sleep at night). I was on my way to visit Rosie, one of the most beloved members of our church family. Rosie was in her mid-eighties and had only been a member for a few years, but she still felt like a matriarchal figure in our church. I was going to visit her because Rosie had been through it, one medical issue after another. A year earlier, she had fallen in her bathroom and broken her arm, and it seemed like it just got worse from there. Over that year, she'd suffered illness from COVID-19; gotten bit by a dog; had pneumonia, a mystery blood clot, chronic obstructive pulmonary disease; and had to watch her beloved St. Louis Cardinals have their worst season in recent memory. She was really struggling.

Rosie had become less and less mobile and was unable to make it to church that Sunday, so I made it a point to go and visit her. When I pulled up to the house, her husband, Anthony, was already waiting for me outside. He hugged me and said, "I'm so glad you came over today" (with a tone that implied that he needed a break).

We walked together into the house, where we were greeted by their cocker spaniel, Duke, who was very excited to have a visitor. As Duke repeatedly jumped up my leg to my chest, I navigated my way to where Rosie was sitting and sat down in the chair next to her. She smiled and wasted no time. "I'm really struggling right now, Pastor Wes. I mean, this is hell."

Not knowing exactly what to say—usually I get a little time for small talk before we jump right to the "God is with you" part of the conversation—I simply replied, "Yeah, well, it sure isn't heaven."

Rosie smiled and laughed and quickly changed the subject. We went through each of her great-grandchildren and how well they were doing in sports. We talked about how things were going in church and the sound quality of our church's live stream, which was a work in progress at the time. Anthony played host a little, bringing me a cold Coca-Cola (which I gratefully accepted), but he mostly just listened to the conversation from across the room.

Then Rosie began to tear up. "It's been really hard for me lately, Pastor. I mean, I've been through some hard stuff before but nothing like this, nothing like what I've been through lately. I've been trying really hard to pray, but I just don't know about that these days."

I leaned in and held her hand. I felt like there really weren't any words that would have helped, so I just kept listening. She paused, and then the tears started to flow. In a cracked voice, she said, "Sometimes when I am really struggling, I just get so mad, and a few times, when I tried to pray, I heard a voice—like a real voice; it's kind of scary—and it says to me, 'Be still and know that I am God!' What is that, Pastor? Where is that coming from?"

Recognizing the verse immediately, I said, "Well, that's from Psalm 46." I waited a beat to see if she already knew that. After a pause, I picked up her Bible that was sitting on her coffee table. It was observably worn and obviously well-used. I thumbed to the middle of the large leather-bound book and found the forty-sixth Psalm, seeing that she'd read it before, for it was highlighted. I read aloud:

He says, "Be still, and know that I am God;
I will be exalted among the nations,
I will be exalted in the earth."
The Lord Almighty is with us;
the God of Jacob is our fortress. (Ps 46:10–11)

Rosie sat wide-eyed for a moment, then grabbed the Bible from me and read it for herself. Staring for a moment, she said, "Wow. I highlighted that in 2004." Apparently, I'd missed the note in the margin that had a date jotted down.

Unlikely as it was that she hadn't heard that Scripture since 2004, in any case, she had forgotten all about it. She was baffled that this word she kept hearing, a word that somehow both comforted and frightened her, was actually from the Bible. "Well, what do you think it means?" she asked. With a little veiled skepticism about people hearing voices, I gave her my best answer: "Well, I think that might be the Holy Spirit, perhaps reminding you that you don't have to try to be God. You don't have to worry; you can simply trust. It takes a lot of trust to be able to sit still in the middle of a lot of chaos, especially the kind of stuff you've been going through."

"Well, maybe it's God telling me to shut my mouth," Rosie said. "That's putting it more bluntly," I replied, "but yeah, that's kinda what I was getting at." We both laughed, and then we prayed together.

STOP TRYING AND START RECEIVING

The definition we most often think of when we think of prayer is probably "when we talk to God." This is the definition I once offered to some children at our church. At our church, like many other churches, we do a Children's Message once a month. The children are invited to come up to the front of the sanctuary and sit on the steps in front of the altar with me for an eight- to ten-minute mini sermon. On this particular Sunday, I was joined on the steps by about nine children, all excited to be there and fascinated by my big poofy robe. My message was about prayer, and I asked the kids if they knew what prayer meant. "It's what we do before we eat snack," one of the preschoolers said, followed by a swell of laughter from the adults in the room. "It's talking to God?" another said with an inquisitive tone, apparently unsure of her answer.

"Yes," I exclaimed. "It's when we talk to God," and I hadn't planned on saying much more about the definition before launching into a quick explanation of the Lord's Prayer from Matthew 6. But just as the words left my mouth, I felt an instant sense of dissatisfaction. That couldn't be it, could it? Is prayer only our talking to God? So I clarified with the following, not quite knowing exactly what I was saying, learning on the spot right along with the kids: "Prayer is also when God listens to us. And God always listens to us. So we can always pray, even if we don't have words." I'm not sure any of the kids thought that was so profound, but for me, it was a revelation. What if we thought of prayer as God's act of listening before we thought of it as *our* act of talking?

As Andrew Prevot has put it, "God is the one who desires first, and with an infinitely greater intensity, to draw close to the beloved. God pines for us and makes this yearning known through revelation; in this sense, God also prays to us."[1] If this is the primary definition of prayer, if it is God's listening to us before it is our talking to God, then God is the primary agent, and we are secondary participants. This means that prayer is not a discipline.

In prayer, "we come with empty hands as well as open hands. What happens is all of grace."[2] Most of the discussions of Christian practices, written from an Aristotelian *poiesis* perspective, focus on human self-actualization and prayer's status as a "spiritual discipline." But I tend to think that *spiritual* and *discipline* are actually mutually exclusive terms, at least from a Christian theological point of view. Discipline is often framed as a skill that requires ongoing effort and refinement. Mastery involves setting clear objectives, practicing regularly, and gradually overcoming challenges. In contemporary self-help literature, authors such as Angela Duckworth in *Grit* highlight the importance of perseverance and effort in cultivating discipline to achieve excellence.[3] The concept of deliberate practice is central to understanding discipline in this context. According to psychologist K. Anders Ericsson, mastering a discipline requires focused, intentional practice aimed at improving performance.[4] This practice is not merely repetitive but also involves feedback and adjustments to continually push one's limits. In late modernity, as Byung-Chul Han points out, the concept of discipline emerges not from a "disciplinary society," which is content to tell us "no, you can't," but from an "achievement society" that replaces "prohibitions, commandments, and the law" with "projects, initiatives, and motivation. . . . The social unconscious switches from *Should* to *Can*."[5] The primary societal pressure has shifted from a negative "you should do this" mentality to a positive "you can do this" mentality, often resulting in a culture of self-exploitation and burnout as individuals push themselves to achieve more based on perceived potential rather than external expectations. A discipline is not only something in which we *should* engage, because of an external value and as an option among many, but also something we *can* and must master in order to reach our potential. This sets discipline apart from mere action. Action, of course, is good (or at least morally neutral), but discipline pushes, coerces, demands, dominates, and expands. Everything becomes a challenge. Discipline imbues action with power, with control, with mastery. We *can*, so we feel guilty if we don't. Discipline in this modernist, postindustrial view is framed as a complex, multifaceted skill that combines consistent practice, intentional focus, and self-management strategies. Mastery of any discipline not only reflects individual effort but also requires the cultivation of a mindset geared toward continuous improvement (i.e., developmentalism) and resilience.

Is prayer really a discipline? Can discipline be spiritual? According to John Calvin, "Genuine prayer is not that by which we arrogantly extol ourselves before God or set a great value on anything of our own."[6] Spirituality is not something to be engineered or controlled through disciplines but rather an immersive experience of resonance that can never be mastered, only encountered—sorta like a relationship. "We must never be discouraged by our lack of prayer," writes Richard Foster. "Even in our prayerlessness we can hunger for God. If so, the hunger itself is prayer."[7] Practices often labeled as *spiritual disciplines*, such as prayer, can be reductive if treated merely as tasks to be mastered. Instead, they should be understood as invitations to engage in a deeper relationship with God and the world around us. Consequently, the term *spiritual discipline* becomes an oxymoron, as it implies a mechanistic approach to something inherently dynamic and relational. As Foster puts it, "Some people work at the business of praying with such intensity that they get spiritual indigestion."[8]

Rather, as we've discussed over the course of this book, prayer is a response to the divine resonance experienced in moments of genuine connection. This understanding shifts the focus from performance and mastery to a more organic participation in the unfolding of spiritual life, emphasizing openness to God's presence rather than adherence to structured practices. Prayer is not something we can just "do better." According to Paul Tillich, "Those amongst us who act as if they knew how to pray, do not know at all."[9] This perspective aligns with contemporary theological reflections that prioritize relationality over rigid structures, inviting individuals to experience spirituality as a fluid, spontaneous, responsive, and surprising interaction with the divine rather than a set of prescribed actions to be diligently followed.

If prayer is to become more than just a source of guilt and shame in a secular age, it has to be removed from the category of discipline and placed in the categories of play or gift. We need to stop "trying" to pray and start receiving prayer. The position of the receiver is the position of dependence, and according to David E. Jenkins, "the ultimate hope of fulfillment and freedom . . . lies in our total dependence."[10] Receptivity leads to playfulness and joy because it opens us to the unexpected, inviting us to engage with life without the need for control or mastery. When we are receptive, we allow ourselves to freely encounter what's around us, experiencing delight in moments as they unfold rather than shaping them to our own ends. This openness lets joy and playfulness arise naturally, as gifts rather than achievements: "In playing we can anticipate our liberation and with laughing rid ourselves of the bonds which alienate us from real life."[11] Prayer is something we receive because it draws us into an experience beyond our own control, where we encounter the sacred rather than directing it. Unlike tasks we manage or outcomes we engineer, prayer invites us to listen and respond, entering into a resonance that flows through us rather than from us. In this way, prayer is not something we produce; it's a gift we receive, inviting us into connection rather than control.

In his short but profound work *Theology and Joy*, Jürgen Moltmann explores how joy and play intersect with theology, offering a perspective that can also reframe prayer. "Play has become a theoretical problem," he writes, "only since man has been forced into disciplined, rationalized labour in constantly growing industrial complexes and since playfulness has been banned from the realm of labour as mere foolishness."[12] Moltmann argues that true joy embodies freedom and the spontaneity of life, qualities often diminished by rigid discipline. If we see prayer through this lens, it can be understood as an act of play rather than a disciplined routine. Playfulness, according to Moltmann, brings us into an unstructured, creative engagement with God that is not bound by performance or achievement but is open, responsive, and deeply resonant.

From Moltmann's perspective, a world that is engineerable and controllable is a dead world, a joyless world. When everything is valued for its usefulness, time becomes a commodity that can be spent or saved like money.[13] Activity that isn't about outcomes is considered "wasted activity," and thus prayer is seen as a "waste of time": "People have lost their capacity for leisure; they no longer know how to do nothing."[14] But it is precisely in the "wasted" time that we discover the true value of human life, not in its usefulness but in what Moltmann calls (quoting Frederik Jacobus Johannes Buytendijk) "the demonstrative value of being."[15] When viewed from an instrumentalist perspective, prayer can seem like a waste of time because it doesn't produce immediate, tangible results or measurable outcomes. Prayer is "for nothing," and to modernity, this is a cause for despair. But for the Christian, it is a source of joy. "'It's all *for nothing* anyway,' says the nihilist and falls into despair," writes Moltmann. "'It's really all *for nothing*,' says the believer, rejoicing in the grace which he can have for nothing and hoping for a new world in which all is available and may be had *for nothing*."[16] Elsewhere he writes, "Where everything must be useful and used, faith tends to regard its own freedom as goods for nothing. It tries to make itself useful and in so doing often gambles away its freedom."[17] Yet this very act of "wasting time" with God, free from productivity or utility, is what can lead us to true freedom. According to Moltmann, "We do not pray freely if need has taught us to pray."[18] By releasing our grip on control and allowing ourselves to simply be in God's presence, we step outside the demands of efficiency and accomplishment. In this unhurried openness, we experience liberation—a freedom that arises not from doing or achieving but from being fully receptive.

In reframing prayer as a gift, Moltmann shifts the focus from our efforts to "get it right" to God's generosity in welcoming us into a relationship. This perspective releases prayer from any sense of pressure or need to achieve a specific outcome, and instead it becomes an opportunity to rest in God's presence. Seen as a gift, prayer allows us to embrace God's grace and enjoy communion without the burden of measurable success, aligning with Moltmann's broader theological stance on joy as a natural and unearned aspect of faith.

THE "PARADOX OF PRAYER"

Henri Nouwen writes, "The paradox of prayer is that we have to learn how to pray while we can only receive it as a gift."[19] Prayer is something we do, but it is also definitively something that God does in us. The axiom employed by Andrew Purves to describe ministry can equally be applied to prayer: "Is [prayer] something we do, or is [prayer] something Jesus does? The answer, of course, is Yes."[20] Prayer is a theological act, to its core. What makes prayer *prayer*—and not just one's talking to oneself or listening to nothing—is that God acts.

According to Paul Tillich, as a human action, prayer is actually an impossibility: "Whether at the right time or not, whether a formulated or a spontaneous prayer, the question is decisive whether prayer is possible at all. . . . This we should never forget when we pray: We do something humanly impossible."[21] The paradox of prayer is that it is something only God can do, and yet, as such, it is something human beings do: "The essence of prayer is the act of God who is working in us and raises our whole being to Himself [*sic*]."[22]

So when we pray, we must remember that we are not the initiators of the conversation. Jesus does not wait at the end of a path called *prayer.* Jesus stands, waiting for us, at the beginning, before we have even a thought to pray. We do not control the Spirit nor coerce God into listening to us. Prayer is a register of grace. It is a gift. So do not enter prayer with shame. Do not enter prayer with guilt. Do not enter prayer with the anxiety that you should try to "master" it as a discipline. But enter prayer with thanksgiving (Ps 100:4). Receive it as a loving invitation. And do not expect God to be disappointed in you, but know and trust that when you come to God—whether you pray alone or with others—you are coming as God's beloved.

THE ANATOMY OF AGENCY

How can we trust that God is listening to us? And what of human agency? Am I suggesting that Christians should stop their work of evangelism and activism? In putting us "on the receiving end" of prayer, am I calling the church to quietism?[23] Am I asking the church to retreat from the public sphere, from community involvement and social justice? That certainly is not my intention. Indeed, by removing prayer from the category of discipline and reframing it as a gift, it is my hope to liberate us from the paralysis of the *should* of achievement society and actually open up the possibility of *more* action—faithful, liberated, and playful action, not discipline. As Moltmann has put it, prayer "does not mean estrangement from action; it is preparation for public, political discipleship."[24] Therefore, offering "thoughts and prayers" must lead to concrete action and participation in God's ongoing work of justice and equity. "For faith," wrote Dietrich Bonhoeffer, "is only real when there is obedience, never without it, and faith only becomes faith in the act of obedience."[25] Indeed, "faith without works is dead" (James 2:26). But the paradox of Christian discipleship is that it is humanly impossible and is only made possible by God's action and on God's side of the equation. As Bonhoeffer writes, "Discipleship is not an offer man makes to Christ. It is only the call which creates the situation."[26]

To better understand this, we need a deeper understanding of agency and how it works. Agency is the capacity of individuals or groups to make choices and act independently, influencing their own circumstances and environment. I have suggested already that divine agency, God's action, is *primary*, and human participation is *secondary*—indeed, it is impossible on its own. But to some, this may not be persuasive. By rendering human agency secondary and thus *unnecessary* from the vantage point of cause and effect, some may think I am relegating human agency to nonimportance. I wish to argue quite the contrary. Because human agency is unnecessary in the face of divine faithfulness, because it stands under the grace of God, which "knocks us flat," our response is of *fundamental* importance.[27] We are indeed under the spell of late modern instrumental rationality if we believe that something needs to be *necessary* in order for it to be important. The human act of prayer is more important to God in the categories of love and resonance than it ever was in the human categories of control and necessity.

Let's consider the anatomy of agency in theological perspective. Anatomy examines how organs, tissues, bones, and other bodily structures are organized, interrelated, and function within the body. An anatomy of agency will examine how divine and human agency are organized, interrelated, and function with respect to their relationship with each other. Another term for what we're examining here is *concursus Dei*—the Christian doctrine referring to the cooperation, or concurrence, of God in human actions and events.

In the first two chapters of Genesis, we are given poetic descriptions of God's creative work. God gathers the dust of the earth, piles it up, and breathes the Spirit of life into it. The human being is made from the dust. Genesis 2:7 states, "Then the Lord God formed the man [*ha'adam*] from the dust of the ground [*adamah*]." This verse highlights that the human being (*adam*) is intrinsically tied to the *adamah*, or soil. By creating humanity from soil, the text portrays human beings as "soil creatures"—beings whose origin, existence, and sustenance are linked to the earth.[28] As soil creatures, humans are, from the outset, portrayed as passive recipients of divine action, "totally dependent upon God,"[29] rather than initiators. The soil itself, in an agricultural context, does not act but is acted upon by the gardener. It receives nutrients, water, and care, which enables it to bring forth life. Similarly, the human creature in Genesis is formed by God's hands, brought to life by God's breath, and placed in a garden prepared and cultivated by God (Gen 2:8). In this sense, humanity is "acted upon" by God in an ongoing, nurturing relationship, even though from this essential passivity, human beings are called to have "dominion" and act upon the soil (Gen 1:26). Humans are passive recipients of divine action, and any "dominion" human beings have is given to them as a gift. Humans are, in a word, dependent.

Just as soil requires external input to yield growth, so humans are dependent on God's provision for life, wisdom, and purpose. Humanity's agency and work in the garden (Gen 2:15) do not originate autonomously but are responsive to God's creative act and ongoing sustenance. This portrayal of the human as passively and fully dependent on God can be understood as an early image of grace: Humanity's existence and sustenance are a gift, and humans remain, in many ways, playful recipients of God's sustaining love. All this means that human agency itself, as a register of theological anthropology, comes under the heading of grace. Our agency is a gift. The human, as a soil creature, is passive to begin with. God is *the* agent. Human beings have done nothing to earn creation. This thread of passivity runs, as it were, throughout the narrative of human existence. In the same way that humans do not earn or achieve their own birth, they do not earn their rebirth, as we see in places like John 3. As the apostle Paul wrote, "For it is by grace you have been saved, through faith—and this is not from yourselves, it is the gift of God—not by works, so that no one can boast" (Eph 2:8–9 NIV). Salvation history is part and parcel to our anthropology, as those who are acted upon by God.

John Swinton asks the very important question "What then can humanity do to reconcile itself with God and begin to move towards His original intentions for them?" His answer reflects the radical passivity that characterizes humans as soil creatures: "Humankind cannot do anything to re-constitute its broken relationship with God!" He writes, "If the relationship between God and humanity is to be restored, the initiative can *only* come from God."[30] Human agency, however we conceive it, must be conceived only after this passivity is established.

Bonhoeffer made this point clear in an address presented in Barcelona in December 1928: "Ethics and religion lie in the direction of human beings to God," he said. "Christ, however, speaks alone, entirely alone, of the direction of God to human people; not of the human way to God but of the way of God to human beings."[31] Human activity itself, then, must run paradoxically in the direction of God to people, not the other way around. God moves toward people, and we are invited to move with God. This is the way of the cross, the anthropology of the cross. Or as Bonhoeffer says, "The Christian idea is the way of God to people and has as the visible objectification of this, the cross."[32]

The anthropology of modernity, however, is an anthropology of glory, an anthropology of achievement. Like Erik Erikson, modernity insists that we become the "self-made man." But according to the gospel, human beings are those who receive their identity and their value, not from their own productivity or action but from God and God alone. Human *being* is not a product of human *becoming* or of human *doing*. As Moltmann puts it, "There is no way to get from doing to being. What man [*sic*] is in his ground precedes what he does and manifests itself in his actions."[33]

To best understand the anatomy of agency, we have to understand God. Further, from a Christian perspective, to understand God, we have to understand, or at least name the mystery of, the anatomy of the Trinity. The Trinity is a central doctrine in Christianity that describes God as one being in three distinct persons: the Father, the Son (Jesus Christ), and the Holy Spirit. Each person of the Trinity is fully and equally God, sharing the same divine essence, yet they are distinct in their relationships and roles. God the Father is often seen as the creator and sustainer of all, the source of all life and existence. God the Son, Jesus Christ, is God with us, incarnate in human form to reveal God and for God to indwell human experience. God the Holy Spirit is present and active in the world, guiding, empowering, and sanctifying creation. The idea of the Trinity addresses the human experience of God as both a unity and a relational being. It emphasizes that God's nature is relational, existing in a perfect relationship of love and unity. While the Trinity is a mystery that can never be fully understood, it is foundational to the Christian faith and shapes Christian worship, prayer, understanding of God's nature and a proper understanding of human action and agency. The *concursus Dei* itself must be understood as trinitarian. Our very humanity is God's before it is ours. Thus, the union between us and God provides the theological texture of ministry and prayer. Even when it becomes a human act by the person being caught up into the life and being of God—and only after that life and being of God is sufficiently free and belongs to God's being God in Godself—it is only ours as a register of our being "nothing" without God (John 15): our abiding.

The corollary of human agency is death. That is the one universal outcome of every human action. We all die (sorry to break it to you). As my good friend and former pastor Ed Davis used to say, "None of us are getting out of this alive." But it is through God's trinitarian agency, the act of God's loving three-in-oneness, that we are swept up off our feet, as it were, and into the divine life, that our being, and only secondarily our doing, has any meaning or purpose.[34] It is only through the divine act of the Father raising the Son from death to life through the power of the Spirit that human life is made real. Only through being taken into and following the death-to-life pattern of Christopraxis is human agency given its value and efficacy through the Holy Spirit. "The divine and human," writes Andrew Root, "are associated not through practices, culture, or even doctrine, but through death."[35] According to Craig Keen, "The gospel insists that it is in his [Christ's] *glorified* dead and damned body that *we*, too, are called to move; that it is in that life that we come alive, that we are saved; that there we repeat (derivatively) his life-rhythm of crucifixion/resurrection."[36] We call this *sanctification*.

Sanctification can be seen as God's ongoing work in taking our flawed human efforts and transforming them into something good. Instead of our own striving to become holy, sanctification is the grace-filled process where God brings value and purpose to our imperfect actions. Human agency is "nothing" outside of sanctification. As such, the work of sanctification is like the work of creation and justification, a free and gracious act of God, making something from nothing—*ex nihilo*. Jesus said, "I am the vine, you are the branches. Those who abide in me and I in them bear much fruit, because apart from me you can do *nothing*" (John 15:5).

One of the clearest and most important treatments of the question of human agency as it relates to God's agency is offered by Kathryn Tanner in her book *Christ the Key*. She writes, "The essentially social character of human persons is an analogue for the essentially relational character of persons within the trinity."[37] Christ, as God with us, becomes the paradigm for human agency. Jesus Christ is both fully divine and fully human in one person. Human being and human experience are taken up into the being of God, and God's being is thus shared with human beings, bridging the divide between the divine and human without evacuating their distinction.

This concept of the union of divine and human being brought together in Christ is called the *hypostatic union* and was formally defined at the Council of Chalcedon in 451 CE, which affirmed that Jesus is "truly God and truly man," possessing all aspects of divinity and humanity. It is through the hypostatic union that human beings are saved. As Gregory of Nazianzus wrote in Epistle 101 to Cledonius the Priest Against Apollinarius, "For that which he has not assumed he has not healed, but that which is united to his Godhead is also saved." This apostolic principle in Christology holds that if Jesus did not take on a human nature like ours, then he was not truly human, and we are not truly saved. It is by being taken up into the Godhead with the second person of the Trinity, Jesus Christ, that we find our true humanity. What we discover is that, just like it has been from the very beginning, we do not achieve our humanity; rather, it is gifted to us. Taken up into God's life and being through the hypostatic union, our humanity belongs to God and is gifted back to us through the sanctifying work of the Holy Spirit.

Likewise, our agency is only ours insofar as it is gifted to us: "The way of God to people leads back to God."[38] God's action always precedes human action. As Tanner puts it, "The Word has united itself with our humanity by way of the hypostatic unity of the incarnation before any change in our own attitudes and dispositions comes to reflect that fact."[39] Being taken up into God's life and being through the hypostatic union, our *agency* belongs to God and is gifted back to us through the sanctifying work of the Holy Spirit. "God is the absolute good," writes Tanner, "not a limited one."[40] Therefore, human beings cannot celebrate any priority in their own action. Indeed, no one can boast: "One cannot congratulate oneself for doing what created powers enable since we are not responsible for the fact that we have those powers to begin with."[41] Tanner continues, "The fundamental reason, in short, why we cannot glory in our achievements is that the power by which we do them remains God's."[42] Human action, then, is passive and derivative, but it is no less important—nor, paradoxically, is it less active.

The theological notion of "passive" action—of being acted upon by God—can be seen as liberating because it reframes human existence away from a relentless pursuit of productivity and achievement and toward an openness to divine grace. In a world that often measures worth through productivity, the idea of passive action resists this norm, emphasizing that true transformation and purpose are found in what we receive rather than in what we achieve. This passivity doesn't denote a lack of vitality or purpose; rather, it repositions us to receive grace that reorients and redefines our identity, purpose, and sense of worth.

As Tanner puts it, "Christ's own life provides not just the pattern of a new human way of life for our imitation, but the cause of that pattern in us, by way of the uniting of humanity and divinity in him . . . It is by being bound to the incomprehensible in and through Christ . . . that we will one day come to live a boundlessly full and good human life."[43] This form of liberated action is inherently freeing because it releases people from the anxieties of performance and accomplishment that often drive modern life. Instead of being shackled to productivity, our worth is rooted in a divine encounter that requires nothing from us. Paradoxically, this reception of grace—a process we do not control but simply participate in—can be profoundly motivating. When we experience God acting upon us, we're moved to act not out of duty or self-interest but out of an overflow of gratitude.

Liberated action caught up in grace, therefore, becomes more motivating, not less motivating, because it springs from a place of joy and assurance rather than from anxiety or obligation. In this state, human action shifts from "I must" to "I may," transforming our engagement with the world. Rather than seeing work and relationships as tasks to complete, they are seen as gifts to be embraced, thus allowing us to act not as laborers but as participants, friends, in God's ongoing work. According to Moltmann, "Christian life or piety . . . must then be described as categories radically different from those which denote man's [*sic*] bondage to the laws of achievement with their compulsions to act. The so-called *new obedience* is *new* only when it is no longer obedience but free, imaginative and loving action."[44] This grace-filled action is thus deeply resonant; it taps into an inexhaustible source of purpose and can fuel a genuinely life-giving, sustaining motivation that transcends any temporary achievement.

THE LIBERATED ACT OF PRAYER

As Sarah Coakley argues persuasively in *The New Asceticism*, human participation in prayer is participation in a "ceaseless dialogue between Spirit and 'Father,'" into which the human being is "caught up" as only one aspect of prayer's very nature.[45] The nature of prayer is trinitarian. As Coakley writes, "The 'Father' (so-called here) is both source and ultimate object of divine longing in us; the 'Spirit' is that irreducibly, though obscurely, distinct enabler and incorporator of that longing in creation (that which *makes* the creation divine; and the 'Son' is that divine and perfected creation, into whose life I, as pray-er, am caught up."[46] The "work" of prayer is only ours because it is first God's and is gifted back to us through God's taking up our experience into the life and being of God through Christ.

We are not compelled to pray; rather, we are invited to let prayer happen to us: "Leaving non-cluttered space for the Spirit is the absolute precondition for the unimpeded flowing of this divine exchange in us."[47] We are invited not to force or achieve anything but to be caught up into the uncontrollability of the divine relational dance that is the Trinity. We are invited not to *do* but to *be* in Christ, to abide, and to let God act upon us. We are invited into prayer as the practice of abiding in God's agency, to cry out with our spirit in the Spirit of God, "Amen."

Jesus said, "If anyone would come after me, let him deny himself and take up his cross daily and follow me" (Luke 9:23 ESV). In Galatians, Paul wrote, "I have been crucified with Christ. It is no longer I who live, but Christ who lives in me. And the life I now live in the flesh I live by faith in the Son of God, who loved me and gave himself for me" (Gal 2:20 ESV). This death to self is profoundly misunderstood if our conclusion is that we shouldn't bother to do anything. Indeed, in the paradigm of John 15, apart from Christ we can indeed "do nothing," but in Christ, being taken up into the life and being of God's trinitarian love through the hypostatic union, we "bear fruit."

The apostle Paul was worried, it seems, about this potential misunderstanding. In Romans chapter 6, he clarifies that the derivative nature and basic passivity of human agency should not lead us to conclude that there is no such thing as human agency or that our work does not matter. Romans 6 is particularly aimed at correcting potential misunderstandings about grace. Paul anticipates that some might misinterpret the radical message of grace as a license to continue sinning: "What shall we say then? Are we to continue in sin that grace may abound? By no means! How can we who died to sin still live in it?" (Rom 6:1–2 NIV). This misconception would undermine the transformative purpose of the gospel, reducing grace to mere forgiveness without real change. Paul wrote to clarify that grace not only forgives but also liberates and empowers believers to live differently, breaking the grip of sin and enabling a life of true freedom in Christ:

> Do you not know that all of us who have been baptized into Christ Jesus were baptized into his death? We were buried therefore with him by baptism into death, in order that, just as Christ was raised from the dead by the glory of the Father, we too might walk in newness of life. For if we have been united with him in a death like his, we shall certainly be united with him in a resurrection like his. We know that our old self was crucified with him in order that the body of sin might be brought to nothing, so that we would no longer be enslaved to sin. For one who has died has been set free from sin. Now if we have died with Christ, we believe that we will also live with him. We know that Christ, being raised from the dead, will never die again; death no longer has dominion over him. For the death he died he died to sin, once for all, but the life he lives he lives to God. So you also must consider yourselves dead to sin and alive to God in Christ Jesus. (Rom 6:3–11 NIV)

Paul is perhaps clearer than I can hope to be that our work is not in vain just because it is fundamentally a gift of grace. On the contrary, because it is gifted to us by God, our work of justice, mercy, generosity, kindness, hospitality, and prayer—all acts that would, as merely human acts, lead only to death—can, as divine acts gifted to us (and thus made genuinely ours), lead from death to life in resurrection through the sanctifying power of God's eternal Spirit.

If prayer were merely a human action, it would be fragile and fleeting—as fragile and fleeting as our own belief. The possibility of prayer would be dependent on *our ability* to pray. It would have to stand on our own strength and our limited (in)ability to control the world around us. It would sway with the tides of circumstance, rising and falling with our own uncertainties. But because prayer is a divine act—an act in which God invites us to join—it stands firm. It doesn't falter when we do, and it isn't shaken by our doubts or fears. Instead, it's held steady by God's own faithful presence, offering us a constant, unshakable connection to the one who sustains all things. Thus, the genuine human act of prayer is a fruit-bearing act precisely because it is first and foremost a divine act. As the primary agent in prayer, the God who raised Jesus from the grave abides in us, and we are invited to abide in God. Prayer is, through Christ, fundamental to the life of the human being. Through it, we can find life. Through surrendering our means to God's ends, through abiding in the "amen" that trusts in the power of God, we can find liberation, hope, and the peace that passes understanding.

Abiding in Breath

Breathing is not a discipline. It doesn't require us to "try" to do it or "get better" at it. Breathing happens to us, more than it is something we do. Breathing, in fact, is something we'd have to try *not* to do if we didn't want to do it. And we wouldn't be able to live without receiving our breath.

Breath prayer is a simple yet profound practice that combines the rhythm of your breath with the invocation of God's presence. This ancient spiritual practice draws from the traditions of the Desert Fathers and Mothers, early Christian ascetics who retreated into the Egyptian desert in the third and fourth centuries. These men and women sought a life of solitude and prayer, aspiring to cultivate a continuous connection with God.

The Desert Fathers and Mothers believed that true prayer could happen in every moment, irrespective of external circumstances. They believed that, like breathing, prayer can be something that happens so naturally that it's more like something that happens *to* us than something we do. They discovered that, in silence and solitude, they could attune themselves to God's unceasing presence and listening ear. This understanding led them to develop short, simple prayers—often referred to as *Jesus prayers*—that could be repeated throughout the day. The aim was to create a rhythm of prayer that allowed them to maintain an awareness of God in their everyday lives that was as close and real as breath itself.

Breath prayer aligns with this tradition by linking a prayer or phrase to the inhalation and exhalation of breath. As you breathe in and out, you focus your mind and heart on God, fostering a deeper awareness of God's presence and love.

STEP-BY-STEP INVITATION TO BREATH PRAYER

1. *Find a Quiet Space*
   Choose a comfortable and quiet place where you can sit or stand undisturbed.

2. *Begin to Breathe*
   Gently close your eyes and take a few deep breaths. Inhale through your nose, allowing your abdomen to expand, and exhale slowly through your mouth.
3. *Choose a Prayer Phrase*
   Select a short phrase or Scripture that resonates with you, for example, "Lord Jesus Christ, have mercy on me"; "Be still and know that I am God"; "God, bring peace"; "You are love."
4. *Associate the Phrase with Your Breath*
   Inhale slowly and silently say the first part of your prayer phrase in your mind. For example, while inhaling, you might say, "Lord Jesus Christ," allowing the breath to fill you with the Spirit's presence.
5. *Exhale with the Second Part*
   As you exhale, say the second part of your prayer phrase. Continuing the example, you would exhale while thinking, "Have mercy on me."
6. *Repeat*
   Continue this cycle of breathing and praying. Inhale, focusing on the first part of your phrase; exhale, focusing on the second part. Aim for a gentle rhythm that feels natural to you.
7. *Remain Present*
   If your mind begins to wander, gently bring back your focus to your breath and the prayer phrase. Allow each breath to draw you deeper into God's presence.
8. *Reflect*
   After your breath prayer session, take a moment to reflect on the experience. Notice any feelings, thoughts, or insights that arose during the practice.

Breath prayer invites you into a space of resonance with God, abiding in the Spirit, echoing the ancient longing of the Desert Fathers and Mothers. Prayer is possible at all times, exists at all times, because God listens to us at all times.

Amen.

Bibliography

Alberta, Tim. *The Kingdom, the Power, and the Glory: American Evangelicals in an Age of Extremism*. Mariner Books, 2023.

Anderson, Ray S. *The Shape of Practical Theology: Empowering Ministry with Theological Praxis*. InterVarsity Press, 2001.

Auten, David Arthur. *Leaving God Behind*. Wipf and Stock, 2018.

Barth, Karl. *Prayer*. Westminster John Knox Press, 2002.

Bell, Rob. *Everything Is Spiritual: Finding Your Way in a Turbulent World*. St. Martin's Essentials, 2020.

Bonhoeffer, Dietrich. *A Testament to Freedom*. HarperCollins, 1990.

———. *The Cost of Discipleship*. Touchstone, 1995.

Brueggemann, Walter. *Genesis. Interpretation: A Bible Commentary for Teaching and Preaching*. John Knox Press, 1982.

Buber, Martin. *I and Thou*. Translated by Ronald Gregor Smith. Charles Scribner's Sons, 1958.

Calvin, John. *Institutes of the Christian Religion*, vol. 1., edited by John T. McNeill, translated by Ford Lewis Battles. Westminster Press, 1960.

Coakley, Sarah. *God, Sexuality, and the Self: An Essay 'On the Trinity'*. Cambridge University Press, 2013.

———. *The New Asceticism: Sexuality, Gender and the Quest for God*. Bloomsbury T&T Clark, 2015.

Coles, Robert. *Erik Erikson: The Growth of His Work*. Atlantic Monthly Press, 1970.

Cook, Lauren. *Generation Anxiety: A Millennial and Gen Z Guide to Staying Afloat in an Uncertain World*. Abrams, 2023.

Dawkins, Richard. *The God Delusion*. Houghton Mifflin, 2006.

Dean, Kenda Creasy, Justin Forbes, Abigail Visco Rusert, and Wesley W. Ellis. *Delighted: What Teenagers Are Teaching the Church About Joy*. Eerdmans, 2020.

Dillenberger, John. *Martin Luther: Selections from His Writings*. Anchor Books, 1961.

Duckworth, Angela. *Grit: The Power of Passion and Perseverance*. Scribner, 2016.

Ellis, Wesley W. *Youth Beyond the Developmental Lens: Being over Becoming*. Fortress Press, 2024.

Episcopal Church. *The Book of Common Prayer and Administration of the Sacraments and Other Rites and Ceremonies of the Church: Together with the Psalter or Psalms of David According to the Use of the Episcopal Church*. Oxford University Press, 1990.

Ericsson, K. Anders. *Peak: Secrets from the New Science of Expertise*. Houghton Mifflin Harcourt, 2016.

Ford, Michael. *Wounded Prophet: A Portrait of Henri J. M. Nouwen*. Doubleday, 1999.

Foster, Richard J. *Prayer: Finding the Heart's True Home*. HarperCollins, 1992.

Fromm, Erich. *To Have or to Be?* Harper & Row, 1976.

Friedman, Lawrence Jacob. *Identity's Architect: A Biography of Erik H. Erikson*. Harvard University Press, 1999.

Geertz, Clifford. *The Interpretation of Cultures*. Basic Books, 1973.

Gingrich, F. Wilbur, and Frederick W. Danker. *Shorter Lexicon of the Greek New Testament*. 2nd ed. University of Chicago Press, 1983.

Grenz, Stanley J. *Prayer: The Cry for the Kingdom*. Rev. ed. Eerdmans, 2005.

Gurevitch, Z. D. "The Power of Not Understanding: The Meeting of Conflicting Identities." *Journal of Applied Behavioral Science* 25, no. 2 (1989): 161–173.

Hall, Douglas John. *The Reality of the Gospel and the Unreality of the Churches*. Fortress Press, 2007.

Han, Byung-Chul. *The Burnout Society*. Stanford Briefs, 2015.

———. *The Crisis of Narration*. Translated by Daniel Steuer. Polity, 2024.

Hay, David, with Rebecca Nye. *The Spirit of the Child*. Rev. ed. Jessica Kingsley Publishers, 2006.

Higgins, Michael W., and Kevin Burns. *Genius Born of Anguish: The Life and Legacy of Henri Nouwen*. Paulist Press, 2012.

Holbert, John C. *Telling the Whole Story: Reading and Preaching Old Testament Stories*. Cascade Books, 2013.

Jennings, Timothy R. *The God-Shaped Brain: How Changing Your View of God Transforms Your Life*. Thomas Nelson, 2015.

Keen, Craig. *After Crucifixion*. Cascade, 2013.

Keener, Craig S. *The IVP Bible Background Commentary: New Testament*. InterVarsity Press, 1993.

King, Mike. *Presence-Centered Youth Ministry: Guiding Students into Spiritual Formation*. InterVarsity Press, 2006.

Martin, James. *Learning to Pray: A Guide for Everyone*. William Collins, 2022.

Merton, Thomas. *A Thomas Merton Reader*. Crown Publishing Group, 1974.

Moltmann, Jürgen. *Religion, Revolution, and the Future*. Scribners, 1969.

———. *Theology and Joy*. SCM Press, 1973.

———. *Experiences of God*, translated by Margaret Kohl. Fortress Press, 1980.

———. *The Trinity and the Kingdom: The Doctrine of God*, translated by Margaret Kohl. Harper and Row, 1981.

———. *God in Creation: A New Theology of Creation and the Spirit of God*, translated by Margaret Kohl. Harper & Row, 1985.

———. *The Coming of God: Christian Eschatology*. Fortress Press, 2004.

Newberg, Andrew, and Mark Robert Waldman. *How God Changes Your Brain: Breakthrough Findings from a Leading Neuroscientist*. Ballantine Books, 2009.

Nietzsche, Friedrich. *The Gay Science*. Translated by Walter Kaufmann. Vintage Books, 1974.

Nouwen, Henri J. M. *Reaching Out: The Three Movements of the Spiritual Life*. Doubleday, 1975.

———. *The Wounded Healer: Ministry in Contemporary Society*. Doubleday, 1979.

———. *In the Name of Jesus: Reflections on Christian Leadership*. Crossroad, 1989.

———. *The Return of the Prodigal Son: A Story of Homecoming*. Image Books, 1992.

Odell, Jenny. *How to Do Nothing: Resisting the Attention Economy*. Melville House, 2019.

O'Laughlin, Michael. *God's Beloved: A Spiritual Biography of Henri Nouwen*. Orbis Books, 2004.

Prevot, Andrew. *Thinking Prayer: Theology and Spirituality amid the Crises of Modernity*. University of Notre Dame Press, 2015.

Purves, Andrew. *The Crucifixion of Ministry*. IVP, 2007.

Rohr, Richard. *The Naked Now: Learning to See as the Mystics See*. Crossroad Publishing, 2009.

Root, Andrew. *Revisiting Relational Youth Ministry: From a Strategy of Influence to a Theology of Incarnation*. IVP Books, 2007.

———. *Christopraxis: A Practical Theology of the Cross*. Fortress Press, 2014.

Root, Andrew. *Faith Formation in a Secular Age*. Baker Academic, 2017.

Root, Andrew, and Blair Bertrand. *When Church Stops Working: A Future for Your Congregation Beyond More Money, Programs, and Innovation*. Baker Publishing Group, 2023.

Root, Andrew, and Kenda Creasy Dean. *The Theological Turn in Youth Ministry*. IVP Books, 2011.

Rosa, Hartmut. *Social Acceleration: A New Theory of Modernity*. Columbia University Press, 2013.

———. *Resonance: A Sociology of Our Relationship to the World*. Polity Press, 2019.

———. *The Uncontrollability of the World*, translated by James Wagner. Polity Press, 2020.

Russell, Bertrand. *Why I Am Not a Christian: And Other Essays on Religion and Related Subjects*, edited by Paul Edwards. Simon and Schuster, 1957.

Smith, James K. A. *How (Not) to Be Secular: Reading Charles Taylor*. William B. Eerdmans Publishing Company, 2014.

Swinton, John. *From Bedlam to Shalom: Toward a Practical Theology of Human Nature, Interpersonal Relationships, and Mental Health Care.* Peter Lang, 2000.

———. *Spirituality and Mental Health Care: Rediscovering a "Forgotten" Dimension.* Jessica Kingsley Publishers, 2001.

Swinton, John. *Becoming Friends of Time: Disability, Timefullness, and Gentle Discipleship.* Baylor University Press, 2016.

Swinton, John, and Harriet Mowat. *Practical Theology and Qualitative Research.* SCM Press, 2006.

Tanner, Kathryn. *Christ the Key.* Cambridge University Press, 2010.

Taylor, Charles. *The Explanation of Behaviour.* Routledge & Kegan Paul, 1964.

———. *A Secular Age.* The Belknap Press of Harvard University Press, 2007.

———. *Sources of the Self: The Making of the Modern Identity.* Harvard University Press, 1989.

———. *The Malaise of Modernity.* Anansi Press, 1991.

Tillich, Paul. *The New Being.* Charles Scribner, 1955.

United Methodist Church. *The United Methodist Book of Worship.* The United Methodist Publishing House, 1992.

Volf, Miroslav. *Exclusion and Embrace: A Theological Exploration of Identity, Otherness, and Reconciliation.* Abingdon Press, 1996.

Weise, Sarah. *Instabrain: The New Rules for Marketing to Generation Z.* Published by the author, 2019.

White, David F. *Tending the Fire That Burns at the Center of the World: Beauty and the Art of Christian Formation.* Wipf and Stock, 2022.

Notes

INTRODUCTION: AMEN

1 I recommend Tim Alberta's book on this topic for a clear and succinct documentation on the transformation of Evangelicalism in America and what happens when Christians start believing that they must "win the culture." See Tim Alberta, *The Kingdom, the Power, and the Glory: American Evangelicals in an Age of Extremism* (Mariner Books, 2023).

2 James K. A. Smith, *How (Not) to Be Secular: Reading Charles Taylor* (William B. Eerdmans Publishing Company, 2014), 4.

3 Hartmut Rosa, *The Uncontrollability of the World*, trans. James Wagner (Polity Press, 2020), viii.

4 Hartmut Rosa, "Give Us a Hearing Heart: The Listening Society and Its Enemies," lecture presented at *The Church, the Pastor, and Resonance in an Accelerated Age: Theological Conversations with Hartmut Rosa*, Princeton Theological Seminary, organized by the Center for Barth Studies and Luther Seminary, September 23, 2024, https://barth.ptsem.edu/hartmut-rosa/.

5 See Charles Taylor, *The Malaise of Modernity* (Anansi Press, 1991).

6 Hartmut Rosa, *Social Acceleration: A New Theory of Modernity* (Columbia University Press, 2013).

7 This is closely related to what I have elsewhere called *developmentalism*. See Wesley W. Ellis, *Youth Beyond the Developmental Lens: Being over Becoming* (Fortress Press, 2024).

8 Rosa, *The Uncontrollability of the World*, ix.

9 Friedrich Nietzsche, *The Gay Science*, trans. Walter Kaufmann (Vintage Books, 1974), 181.

10 Andrew Root and Kenda Creasy Dean, *The Theological Turn in Youth Ministry* (IVP Books, 2011), 195.

11 Martin Buber, *I and Thou*, trans. Ronald Gregor Smith (Charles Scribner's Sons, 1958).

12 Erich Fromm, *To Have or to Be?* (Harper and Row, 1976).

13 I am indebted to Andrew Root for this part of the thesis. See Andrew Root, *Revisiting Relational Youth Ministry: From a Strategy of Influence to a Theology of Incarnation* (IVP Books, 2007).

14 Richard Rohr, *The Naked Now: Learning to See as the Mystics See* (Crossroad Publishing, 2009), 23.
15 Rohr, *The Naked Now*, 23.
16 Hartmut Rosa, *Resonance: A Sociology of Our Relationship to the World* (Polity Press, 2019), 1.
17 Andrew Root and Blair Bertrand, *When Church Stops Working: A Future for Your Congregation Beyond More Money, Programs, and Innovation* (Baker Publishing Group, 2023).
18 Joel Coen, dir., *The Big Lebowski* (PolyGram Filmed Entertainment, 1998).
19 Seriously, just go watch the film.
20 Rosa, *The Uncontrollability of the World*, 5–14.
21 Rosa names this tension in his chapter titled "To Take Control or to Let Things Happen?" Rosa, *The Uncontrollability of the World*, 60–85.
22 It should be noted that the more straightforward translation of *anōthen*, the Greek word translated as *again*, is actually *from above* (as the NRSVUE translates it). But *again* is a viable translational option (see Gal 4:9), and according to F. Wilbur Gingrich and Frederick Danker, the word in John 3:3 "is purposely given a double meaning *again* and *from above*." F. Wilbur Gingrich and Frederick W. Danker, *Shorter Lexicon of the Greek New Testament*, 2nd ed. (University of Chicago Press, 1983), 18.
23 Here I am reminded of the theology of presence in works of Mike King and Richard Rohr. See Rohr, *The Naked Now*, and Mike King, *Presence-Centered Youth Ministry: Guiding Students into Spiritual Formation* (InterVarsity Press, 2006).
24 Rosa, *Resonance*, 1.
25 Rohr, *The Naked Now*, 16.
26 Jürgen Moltmann's concept of *perichoresis* draws from the theological tradition of describing the interrelationship within the Trinity. It refers to the dynamic, mutual indwelling and interpenetration of the Father, Son, and Holy Spirit without losing their distinctiveness. For Moltmann, *perichoresis* underscores the relational and communal nature of God, emphasizing a divine unity that is not static or hierarchical but characterized by love, reciprocity, and openness. This relationality extends to creation, suggesting that human and cosmic life is invited to participate in the divine communion, reflecting God's relational being. See Jürgen Moltmann, *The Trinity and the Kingdom: The Doctrine of God*, trans. Margaret Kohl (Harper and Row, 1981), 171–178.
27 Charles Taylor refers to this as the "fragilization" of belief. See Charles Taylor, *A Secular Age* (Belknap Press of Harvard University Press, 2007), 556–557. Andrew Root, building on Taylor, discusses three "symptoms" of secularization, or three "understandings" of the secular: secular one, secular two, and secular three. Secular one refers to the bifurcation of "sacred" and "secular" spaces, secular two refers to "religious versus a-religious spaces" and the weakening of religious institutions (think of the "decline"

of the church). This contestability, or "fragilization" (Taylor), of belief is characteristic of the third understanding or symptom, secular three. See Andrew Root, *Faith Formation in a Secular Age* (Baker Academic, 2017), 103–112. Also see Root and Bertrand, *When Church Stops Working*, 9–12.

CHAPTER 1: I DON'T KNOW HOW TO PRAY

1 Karl Barth, *Prayer* (Westminster John Knox Press, 2002), 13, 19.
2 Barth, *Prayer*, 26.
3 Stanley J. Grenz, *Prayer: The Cry for the Kingdom*, rev. ed. (Eerdmans, 2005), 3.
4 Grenz, *Prayer*, 4.
5 Grenz, *Prayer*, 5.
6 I recently stopped using the language of *service* to describe what we do when we gather on Sunday mornings. It was my friend Rev. Greg Davis, a fellow member of the United Church of Christ, who alerted me to the problem of thinking of worship as a service. Not only does it reduce worship to a resource and a commodity, but it also positions those who gather as recipients rather than participants in the beautiful and intimate experience of worshiping God. So I've consciously switched, as long as I don't forget to do so, to talking about worship as a *gathering* instead of a *service*.
7 Episcopal Church, *The Book of Common Prayer and Administration of the Sacraments and Other Rites and Ceremonies of the Church: Together with the Psalter or Psalms of David According to the Use of the Episcopal Church* (Oxford University Press, 1990), 79.
8 United Methodist Church, *The United Methodist Book of Worship* (The United Methodist Publishing House, 1992), 51.
9 This is an assurance of pardon I often use when I am leading worship liturgy, and while I am sure it's not completely original, I don't think it's a direct quote from any source.

CHAPTER 2: PRAYER IS NOT A MATTER OF FACT

1 Bertrand Russell, *Why I Am Not a Christian: And Other Essays on Religion and Related Subjects*, ed. Paul Edwards (Simon and Schuster, 1957); Richard Dawkins, *The God Delusion* (Houghton Mifflin, 2006).
2 Andrew Prevot, *Thinking Prayer: Theology and Spirituality amid the Crises of Modernity* (University of Notre Dame Press, 2015), 2.
3 Sarah Coakley, *God, Sexuality, and the Self: And Essay 'On the Trinity'* (Cambridge University Press, 2013), 55.
4 Taylor, *A Secular Age* (The Belknap Press of Harvard University Press, 2007), 3.

5 Charles Taylor, *Sources of the Self: The Making of the Modern Identity* (Harvard University Press, 1989)
6 Taylor, *A Secular Age*, 35, 37–38.
7 Taylor, *A Secular Age*, 38.
8 Taylor, *A Secular Age*, 42.
9 Taylor, *A Secular Age*, 543.
10 Taylor, *A Secular Age*, 542.
11 Jürgen Moltmann, *God in Creation: A New Theology of Creation and the Spirit of God*, trans. Margaret Kohl (Minneapolis: Fortress Press, 1993), 2.
12 Moltmann, *God in Creation*, 2.
13 According to David White, "Under the guidance of thinkers like Descartes and Kant, modernity impoverishes us by reducing us to thinking things connected to the world only by thought and for the purpose of mastery." David F. White, *Tending the Fire That Burns at the Center of the World: Beauty and the Art of Christian Formation* (Wipf and Stock, 2022), 5.
14 Andrew Root, *Christopraxis: A Practical Theology of the Cross* (Fortress Press, 2014), 248.
15 Thomas Merton, *A Thomas Merton Reader* (Crown Publishing Group, 1974), 458.
16 Rohr, *The Naked Now*, 15.
17 This idea of future aligns with what Moltmann has called *futurum*, which is to be distinguished from *advenus*—future as the developmental progression of the present into the future as opposed to the coming of God into the present as future. See Jürgen Moltmann, *The Coming of God: Christian Eschatology* (Fortress Press, 2004), 25–26.
18 Jürgen Moltmann, *Religion, Revolution and the Future* (Scribners, 1969), 189.
19 Moltmann, *God in Creation*, 32.
20 Jürgen Moltmann, *Experiences of God*, trans. Margaret Kohl (Fortress Press, 1980), 59.
21 Smith, *How (Not) to Be Secular*, 92.
22 Andrew Root places the blame for this pretty squarely on the shoulders of Aristotle. He writes, "Modernity's man exists squarely in the hubris of the Aristotelean framework of actuality to possibility: the actuality of human instrumental rationality gives shape to reality." Root, *Christopraxis*, 248.
23 Taylor, *A Secular Age*, 32.
24 Taylor, *A Secular Age*, 38.
25 John Swinton and Harriet Mowat, *Practical Theology and Qualitative Research* (SCM Press, 2006), 39–44.
26 John Swinton, *Spirituality and Mental Health Care: Rediscovering a 'Forgotten' Dimension* (Jessica Kingsley Publishers, 2001), 47.
27 See Ellis, *Youth Beyond the Developmental Lens*, 15–28.
28 Clifford Geertz, *The Interpretation of Cultures* (Basic Books, 1973), 89.
29 Smith, *How (Not) to Be Secular*, 93.
30 Taylor, *A Secular Age*, 3.

31 See Rob Bell, *Everything Is Spiritual: Finding Your Way in a Turbulent World* (St. Martin's Essentials, 2020).
32 Taylor, *A Secular Age*, 544.
33 Swinton, *Spirituality and Mental Health Care*, 8.
34 Taylor, *Sources of the Self*, 19.
35 See, for example, Andrew Newberg and Mark Robert Waldman, *How God Changes Your Brain: Breakthrough Findings from a Leading Neuroscientist* (Ballantine Books, 2009), and Timothy R. Jennings, *The God-Shaped Brain: How Changing Your View of God Transforms Your Life* (Thomas Nelson, 2015).
36 Root, *Christopraxis*, 195.
37 Grenz, *Prayer*, 38.
38 See David Hay with Rebecca Nye, *The Spirit of the Child*, rev. ed. (Jessica Kingsley Publishers, 2006), 18–22.
39 David Artur Auten, *Leaving God Behind* (Wipf and Stock, 2018), 23.
40 Hay with Nye, *The Spirit of the Child*, 59.
41 Grenz, *Prayer*, 54.
42 Elsewhere, I have referred to this as the *empiricist regime* in epistemology. See Ellis, *Youth Beyond the Developmental Lens*.
43 Miroslav Volf, *Exclusion and Embrace: A Theological Exploration of Identity, Otherness, and Reconciliation* (Abingdon Press, 1996), 143.
44 Volf, *Exclusion and Embrace*, 143.
45 Z. D. Gurevitch, "The Power of Not Understanding: The Meeting of Conflicting Identities," *Journal of Applied Behavioral Science* 25, no. 2 (1989): 161–73.
46 Volf, *Exclusion and Embrace*, 144.
47 Volf, *Exclusion and Embrace*, 143.
48 Moltmann, *God in Creation*, 32.
49 John Calvin, *Institutes of the Christian Religion*, vol. 1, ed. John T. McNeill, trans. Ford Lewis Battles (Westminster Press, 1960), 61–62.
50 Moltmann writes, "*Belief* in creation only arrives at the understanding of creation when it recollects the alternative forms of *meditative* knowledge. 'We know to the extent to which we love,' said Augustine." Moltmann, *God in Creation*, 32.
51 Andrew Purves, *The Crucifixion of Ministry* (IVP, 2007), 33.

CHAPTER 3: HAUNTED BY TRANSCENDENCE

1 Charles Taylor, *The Explanation of Behaviour* (London: Routledge and Kegan Paul, 1964).
2 Some exemplars in addressing psychology as mystery, and not as a hard science, include William Kessen, Rollo May, Robert D. Stolorow, and Erica Burman.
3 Smith, *How (Not) to Be Secular*, 3–4.

4 Michael O'Laughlin, *God's Beloved: A Spiritual Biography of Henri Nouwen* (Orbis Books, 2004), 25.
5 O'Laughlin, *God's Beloved*, 19
6 Michael Ford, *Wounded Prophet: A Portrait of Henri J. M. Nouwen* (Doubleday, 1999), xi.
7 Michael W. Higgins and Kevin Burns, *Genius Born of Anguish: The Life and Legacy of Henri Nouwen* (Paulist Press, 2012), 23.
8 Ford, *Wounded Prophet*, 5.
9 O'Laughlin, *God's Beloved*, 26
10 O'Laughlin, *God's Beloved*, 38.
11 Ford, *Wounded Prophet*, 87.
12 O'Laughlin, *God's Beloved*, 38.
13 Lawrence Jacob Friedman, *Identity's Architect: A Biography of Erik H. Erikson* (Harvard University Press, 1999), 29.
14 Friedman, *Identity's Architect*, 29.
15 Karla was a strong and loving influence on Erik and was the first of a pattern of strong and intelligent women in Erik's life. He seems to have clung to women like his mother. Later on, it would be Anna Freud, daughter of the famed Sigmund Freud, then his wife Joan, and eventually even Margaret Mead would fill this role in his life.
16 Friedman, *Identity's Architect*, 31.
17 Friedman, *Identity's Architect*, 33.
18 Friedman, *Identity's Architect*, 38.
19 Higgins and Burns, *Genius Born of Anguish*, 23–24.
20 O'Laughlin, *God's Beloved*, 41.
21 O'Laughlin, *God's Beloved*, 41.
22 O'Laughlin, *God's Beloved*, 43.
23 Higgins and Burns, *Genius Born of Anguish*, 29.
24 O'Laughlin, *God's Beloved*, 47.
25 Friedman, *Identity's Architect*, 87–88.
26 Smith, *How (Not) to Be Secular*, 3–4.
27 Robert Coles, *Erik Erikson: The Growth of His Work* (An Atlantic Monthly Press, 1970), 46.
28 Coles, *Erik Erikson*, 36.
29 Henri J. M. Nouwen, *The Wounded Healer: Ministry in Contemporary Society* (Doubleday, 1979).
30 Henri J. M. Nouwen, *The Return of the Prodigal Son: A Story of Homecoming* (Image Books, 1992).
31 Taylor, *A Secular Age*, 548.
32 Friedman, *Identity's Architect*, 209.
33 Friedman, *Identity's Architect*, 219.
34 Friedman, *Identity's Architect*, 218, 219.
35 Friedman, *Identity's Architect*, 219.

36 Henri J. M. Nouwen, *In the Name of Jesus: Reflections on Christian Leadership* (Crossroad, 1989), 19.
37 Nouwen, *In the Name of Jesus*, 20.
38 This is the apt phrase used by Michael O'Laughlin to describe Nouwen's down-to-earth nature. O'Laughlin, *God's Beloved*, 14.
39 We can rightly critique Nouwen's characterization of people with disabilities as "poor in spirit" as disturbingly ableist, but his point should not be lost on us. Nouwen, *In the Name of Jesus*, 22.
40 Again, we're right to note and condemn the ableism of Nouwen's characterization of people with disabilities. Nouwen, *In the Name of Jesus*, 22–23.
41 O'Laughlin, *God's Beloved*, 143.
42 O'Laughlin, *God's Beloved*, 14.
43 O'Laughlin, *God's Beloved*, 177.
44 Taylor, *A Secular Age*, 299–313; Root, *Christopraxis*, 247–252.
45 According to James K. A. Smith, *fragilization* means "in the face of different options, where people who lead 'normal' lives do not share my faith (and perhaps believe something very different), my own faith commitment becomes fragile—put into question, dubitable." Smith, *How (Not) to Be Secular*, 141.

CHAPTER 4: BORN IN THE MALAISE

1 Andrew Root, *The Pastor in a Secular Age* (Baker, 2019), 273.
2 See Kenda Creasy Dean, Justin Forbes, Abigail Visco Rusert, and Wesley W. Ellis, *Delighted: What Teenagers Are Teaching the Church About Joy* (Eerdmans, 2020), and Ellis, *Youth Beyond the Developmental Lens.*
3 Market Realist, "How Gen Z Is Shaping the Future of Work by Embracing Entrepreneurship, Remote Work over Traditional Jobs," accessed December 7, 2024, https://marketrealist.com.
4 Harmony Healthcare IT, "Survey: 42% of Gen Z Diagnosed with a Mental Health Condition," accessed November 11, 2023, https://www.psychiatrist.com/news/survey-42-of-gen-z-diagnosed-with-a-mental-health-condition/.
5 Lauren Cook, *Generation Anxiety: A Millennial and Gen Z Guide to Staying Afloat in an Uncertain World* (Abrams, 2023), 2.
6 Byung-Chul Han, *The Crisis of Narration*, trans. Daniel Steuer (Polity, 2024), x, 14, 62.
7 Han, *The Crisis of Narration*, 24.
8 Han, *The Crisis of Narration*, 2.
9 Han, *The Crisis of Narration*, 2.
10 Sarah Weise, *Instabrain: The New Rules for Marketing to Generation Z* (Independently published, 2019), 10.

11 Rosa, *The Uncontrollability of the World*, 9–10.
12 Rosa, *The Uncontrollability of the World*, 11.
13 James Martin, *Learning to Pray: A Guide for Everyone* (William Collins, 2022), 43–59.
14 Martin, *Learning to Pray*, 59.
15 Martin, *Learning to Pray*, 44, 47.
16 Moltmann, *The Coming of God*, xv–xvi.
17 Dietrich Bonhoeffer, *The Cost of Discipleship* (Touchstone, 1995), 50–51.
18 Root and Bertrand, *When Church Stops Working*, 24.
19 Root and Bertrand, *When Church Stops Working*, 23.
20 Byung-Chul Han, *The Burnout Society* (Stanford Briefs, 2015), 8–11.
21 Rosa, *The Uncontrollability of the World* (Polity Press, 2019), 5–14
22 Rosa, *The Uncontrollability of the World*, 9.
23 Han, *The Burnout Society*, 39.
24 Ellis, *Youth Beyond the Developmental Lens*, 6.
25 Jenny Odell, *How to Do Nothing: Resisting the Attention Economy* (Melville House, 2019), xix.
26 Rosa, *The Uncontrollability of the World*, 59.
27 Fromm, *To Have or to Be?*, 25.
28 According to Rosa, "The basic mode of vibrant human existence consists not in exerting *control* over things but in resonating with them." Rosa, *The Uncontrollability of the World*, 31.
29 Rosa, *The Uncontrollability of the World*, 37.
30 I am borrowing this bird-watching metaphor from a friend and colleague, Marcus Hong, of Louisville Presbyterian Theological Seminary. Years after he shared this metaphor with me, I came across a similar one in Jenny Odell's work. See Odell, *How to Do Nothing*, 7. Hong has also used the metaphor of a trellis. We can put up a trellis and water the garden, but ultimately, we cannot control where the vines will grow.
31 Rosa, *The Uncontrollability of the World*, 51.
32 Rosa, *The Uncontrollability of the World*, 58–59.
33 Coakley, *God, Sexuality, and the Self*, 23.

CHAPTER 5: PLAYING BETTER GAMES

1 I write more about this in *Youth Beyond the Developmental Lens*, 103–107.
2 Craig S. Keener, *The IVP Bible Background Commentary: New Testament* (InterVarsity Press, 1993), 569.
3 Jürgen Moltmann, *Theology of Hope: On the Ground and the Implications of a Christian Eschatology*, trans. James W. Leitch (Fortress Press, 1993), 21.
4 Douglas John Hall, *The Reality of the Gospel and the Unreality of the Churches* (Fortress Press, 2007), 81.
5 Hall, *The Reality of the Gospel*, 81.

6 Hall, *The Reality of the Gospel*, 97.
7 Ray S. Anderson introduced the concept in his book *The Shape of Practical Theology: Empowering Ministry with Theological Praxis* (InterVarsity Press, 2001).
8 Root, *Christopraxis*.
9 According to Andy Root, "The incarnation makes personhood forever the entrance into the transcendent encounter of the divine with the human . . . to have an experience of the *person* of Jesus Christ coming to your *own person*." Root, *Faith Formation in a Secular Age*, 142.

CHAPTER 6: THE PARADOX OF PRAYER

1 Prevot, *Thinking Prayer*, 14.
2 Richard J. Foster, *Prayer: Finding the Heart's True Home* (HarperCollins, 1992), 203.
3 See Angela Duckworth, *Grit: The Power of Passion and Perseverance* (Scribner, 2016).
4 See K. Anders Ericsson, *Peak: Secrets from the New Science of Expertise* (Houghton Mifflin Harcourt, 2016).
5 Han, *The Burnout Society*, 9.
6 John Calvin, *Prayer: The Chief Exercise of Faith*, ed. Dustin Benge (Crossway, 2022), 43.
7 Foster, *Prayer*, 23.
8 Foster, *Prayer*, 23.
9 Paul Tillich, *The New Being* (Charles Scribner's Sons, 1955), 135.
10 David E. Jenkins, "The Liberation of 'God,'" in Jürgen Moltmann, *Theology and Joy* (SCM Press, 1973), 6.
11 Moltmann, *Theology and Joy*, 28.
12 Moltmann, *Theology and Joy*, 29.
13 John Swinton, *Becoming Friends of Time: Disability, Timefullness, and Gentle Discipleship* (Baylor University Press, 2016), 23.
14 Moltmann, *Theology and Joy*, 33–34.
15 Moltmann, *Theology and Joy*, 42.
16 Moltmann, *Theology and Joy*, 54.
17 Moltmann, *Theology and Joy*, 39.
18 Moltmann, *Theology and Joy*, 84.
19 Henri J. M. Nouwen, *Reaching Out: The Three Movements of the Spiritual Life* (Doubleday, 1975), 123.
20 Purves, *The Crucifixion of Ministry*, 52.
21 Tillich, *The New Being*, 136–137.
22 Tillich, *The New Being*, 138.
23 Quietism is a spiritual and theological movement that emphasizes inner stillness, detachment from one's own will, and a passive submission to

God as the path to spiritual perfection. In quietism, the focus is on the soul's total surrender to God's presence, often discouraging active efforts in prayer or moral actions, under the belief that spiritual transformation happens only when one is entirely passive to God's will. Originating with the teachings of Spanish priest Miguel de Molinos in the seventeenth century, quietism advocated for a deep, contemplative stillness free from any striving or human ambition. This approach views human effort as a potential hindrance to union with God, suggesting that God's work in the soul can be obstructed by self-will or personal spiritual efforts. Quietism faced significant criticism, especially from the Roman Catholic Church, which condemned Molinos's teachings as heretical in 1687. Opponents argued that quietism's emphasis on passivity neglected the importance of active virtue, community involvement, and the practices traditionally seen as part of Christian life.

24 Moltmann, *Experiences of God*, 73.

25 Bonhoeffer, *The Cost of Discipleship*, 64.

26 Bonhoeffer, *The Cost of Discipleship*, 63. Bonhoeffer goes on to say, "We must make a definite step. What does this mean? It means that we can only take this step aright if we fix our eyes not on the work we do, but on the word with which Jesus calls us to do it," 66.

27 Kathryn Tanner writes, "Grace knocks us flat, preventing any form of self-congratulation. All the good we achieve is to be attributed to God rather than to ourselves." Kathryn Tanner, *Christ the Key* (Cambridge University Press, 2010), 76.

28 I first heard this term *soil creatures* from Nathan Stucky, quoting Old Testament scholar Jacqueline Lapsley, at the Farminary at Princeton Theological Seminary, but it has been used elsewhere before. See Holbert, *Telling the Whole Story: Reading and Preaching Old Testament Stories* (Cascade Books, 2013), 49–54.

29 Walter Brueggemann, *Genesis* (Interpretation: A Bible Commentary for Teaching and Preaching; John Knox Press, 1982), 45.

30 John Swinton, *From Bedlam to Shalom* (Peter Lang Publishing, 2000), 54–55.

31 Dietrich Bonhoeffer, *A Testament to Freedom* (HarperCollins, 1990), 52.

32 Bonhoeffer, *A Testament to Freedom*, 52.

33 Moltmann, *Theology and Joy*, 66.

34 And indeed the term *purpose* becomes deeply nuanced, if not ironic.

35 Root, *Christopraxis*, 105.

36 Craig Keen, *After Crucifixion* (Cascade, 2013), 28.

37 Tanner, *Christ the Key*, 3.

38 Bonhoeffer, *A Testament to Freedom*, 53.

39 Tanner, *Christ the Key*, 72.

40 Tanner, *Christ the Key*, 49.

41 Tanner, *Christ the Key*, 81.

42 Tanner, *Christ the Key*, 85.

43 Tanner, *Christ the Key*, 57.
44 Moltmann, *Theology and Joy*, 67.
45 Sarah Coakley, *The New Asceticism: Sexuality, Gender, and the Quest for God* (Bloomsbury, 2012), 88–89.
46 Coakley, *The New Asceticism* 90.
47 Coakley, *The New Asceticism*, 91.